The Guide to Welsh Perry & Cider

by **Pete Brown** & **Bill Bradshaw**

Published by Welsh Perry & Cider Society, May 2013

Text and Image Copyright © Welsh Perry & Cider Society Ltd

Design by Mediadesign Ltd www.mediadesign-wales.co.uk

ISBN 978-0-9576561-0-9

Printed in Wales, UK

Foreword

Wales is a nation bursting with good things to eat. It's wonderful to be able to say that with real confidence and it is the result of an extraordinary couple of decades in which small producers - driven by passion and a common commitment to quality - have transformed the food map of the nation. It's a heady mix of innovation and tradition that has brought us the likes of wonderful artisan cheeses, native breed meats, and an overdue recognition of the delicious bounty available from our long coastline.

Good food of course needs an equally worthy partner at the table in the form of something excellent to drink and for me the revival in interest in perry and cider is one of the most exciting developments in recent years in Welsh food. Like much else in the food world the market is dominated by mass production, but a sip of something that speaks of the fruit from which it was made and the love and care bestowed upon it by the makers, is a richer experience altogether.

These gems are well worth searching for and that's why a guide like this is both welcome and necessary. These pages not only open up the world of Welsh perry and cider and point you in the direction to track them down, they also tell the stories behind the golden liquid you find in your glass. It is a sparkling addition to Welsh food and drink culture and a damned good read too. Best enjoyed with a glass of Welsh perry or cider - naturally.

Simon Wright

Food writer, broadcaster, proprietor of Wright's Food Emporium, and former Editor of the AA Restaurant Guide

> 66 the revival in interest in perry and cider is one of the most exciting developments in recent years in Welsh food. 99

Welsh Perry and Cider Society

The Welsh Perry & Cider Society (WPCS) was founded in 2001 as a not-for-profit organisation that aims to promote Welsh cider and perry (made in Wales, ideally from Welsh fruit). We also provide support and assistance to existing and potential Welsh cider makers, as well as researching and regenerating Welsh orchards by helping with the identification and conservation of rare varieties of Welsh cider apples and perry pears.

After a decade of incredible growth in Welsh cider and perry we decided it was time to spread the word about it. But just to make sure we weren't being too biased, we decided to bring in an outside perspective...

Pete and Bill bowled us over with their ideas about how to research and write this guide, and we found them impossible to refuse! Armed with the experience of travelling the globe in search of the gems in the craft cider world, Pete and Bill promised us an exciting, unique view of what Wales has to offer visitors; whether a real cider enthusiast or just someone keen to find out a bit more about our re-emerging tradition.

So what you are about to read is an exploration of cider and perry in Wales from the perspective of two English men with a passion for and knowledge of cider. The views expressed are their own, but we think you'll agree that it's a perspective that just makes you want to get out there and experience what they've experienced, meet some of the interesting characters of the Welsh cider world, and try some of their remarkable wares in some great establishments.

www.welshcider.co.uk

> ❝ After a decade of incredible growth in Welsh cider and perry we decided it was time to spread the word about it. ❞

Cymdeithas
P e r a i
S e i d r
C y m r u

About the Authors

Pete Brown

Pete Brown is one of the UK's leading beer writers, author of four previous books and was named British Beer Writer of the Year in 2009 and 2012. Over the past three years he has expanded his interest into cider and is learning as fast as he can. Together with Bill Bradshaw he is also the author of World's Best Cider, published in October 2013. You can follow Pete's musings at petebrown.blogspot.com

Bill Bradshaw

Bill Bradshaw is a freelance photographer from Somerset who has been passionately documenting cider around the world since 2004 with his award winning work being published internationally. He frequents all corners of the cider world whether shooting personal work, consulting for business or judging cider competitions. His images and travels are documented on his blog: iamcider.blogspot.com

Contents

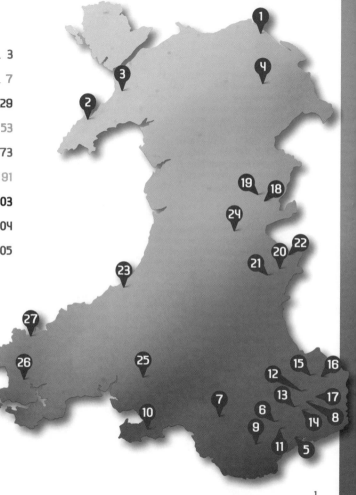

1

Welcome to Wales!

As any rugby fan will tell you, over the last ten to fifteen years Wales has regained its mojo in spectacular style.

Devastated by the loss of its industrial base, the country suffered massively in the late twentieth century. But in the twenty-first it has reinvented itself. With a new Welsh Assembly in 1998, and imaginative investment and funding from various bodies, its city centres have been rejuvenated, and its stunning countryside has helped generate a thriving tourist economy.

Within this, Welsh food and drink plays a vital role. Almost eighty per cent of Wales is farmland, but most of the country is mountainous with soil that's less ideal for crops, so grazing livestock is much more important. Welsh lamb is world-famous, the beef and pork aren't bad either. Dairy farms give us Welsh cheese, of which Caerphilly is best known – there's much more besides, as the wonderfully iconic *Welsh Rarebit* demonstrates.

Farmers have been taking their cattle to market across the mountains and valleys for centuries, and the drovers' inns that sprang up along the roads to offer them shelter and sustenance have evolved into some of the best country pubs in the world. Before anyone had even heard of the word 'gastropub', before good quality restaurants started shouting about how they sourced their produce locally, Welsh pubs were packed with people enjoying restaurant-standard dishes, served by staff who could tell you the name of the cow on your plate, if that didn't make you squeamish.

And over the last ten years, those pubs have seen a startling revolution in the range of Welsh drinks available to them. Welsh brewing got there first, with a craft beer revolution that has seen over fifty brewers spring up all across the country. Less heralded – until now – was the even more dramatic explosion in craft cider making.

> 66 Over the last ten years pubs have seen a startling revolution in the range of Welsh drinks available to them 99

In little more than a decade, cider making in Wales has gone from being a forgotten irrelevance to a thriving scene on a par with Britain's legendary cider regions, Somerset and Herefordshire.

Welsh cider has throughout history been in the shadow of its more famous neighbour, but good apples don't recognise national borders and South Wales in particular has long been noted for its cider. This declined in the late twentieth century, but a few pioneers began experimenting in the late eighties and nineties, generating enough interest to form the Welsh Perry and Cider Society in 2001. The Society now has over forty producer members, from large commercial concerns to hobbyists making a few gallons in the garden shed.

Cider in general is enjoying an amazing boom in popularity, but if your idea of cider extends as far as a pint bottle served with a glass full of ice, you don't know what you've been missing! Cider is a much-misunderstood drink, with an astonishing array of flavours and varieties. And perry – so obscure that many people don't even know what it is – can easily rival the finest champagnes.

We appreciate that not everyone will go so far as to organise a visit to Wales based purely on discovering its cider (though having done so for this book, we would heartily recommend it). But Wales is a wonderful country to explore whatever your tastes, and a glass of Welsh cider, made with 100 per cent pressed apple juice with few or no additives, will make any pub visit or food festival that bit more special. And you can't come to Wales without checking out the pubs or the festivals.

One final, vitally important piece of information before you jump into this guide. Wales is officially a bilingual country. It's always good fun trying to learn a few words of the Welsh language, and there is one that you will definitely need. The Welsh for 'cheers' or literally 'good health' - is 'Iechydd Da!' (pronounced yeh-chid-dah). Get a glass in your hand, and give it a try.

Getting there and getting around

Wales is a mountainous country that's not always easy to get across, but getting there is perfectly straightforward. Cardiff Airport has flights to and from various destinations across the UK and Europe. Manchester, Bristol and Birmingham airports are all close to the Welsh border.

Three quarters of the population live along the bottom of the country, in or around the main population centres of Newport, Cardiff and Swansea. Both the M4 motorway and the First Great Western train line run from London through all three. In the north, the A55 performs a similar role, running all the way from Chester across the border along the north coast. Getting between north and south can be tricky thanks to the three mountain ranges of the Brecon Beacons, Cambrian Mountains and Snowdonia being in the way. The A49 runs up the length of Wales just over the border in England, and is a useful way of getting to some of the less accessible parts of Mid Wales. The Arriva Trains service from Manchester to Cardiff follows a similar route.

If you want to do it the hard way, travelling through Mid Wales, the stunning scenery more than makes up for any difficulty in getting from place to place quickly. The journey itself can be more worthwhile than the destination.

The usual hotel chains are available in all major towns and cities, but to get the most out of Wales it's best to take advantage of the country inns and B&Bs, or the stunning campsites.

For more details on travel and accommodation, we suggest checking out **www.visitwales.co.uk**. **The Rough Guide** and **Lonely Planet Guide to Wales** are also packed full of information and ideas.

An Introduction to Craft Cider and Perry

What is cider?

It's a simple enough question, isn't it? But it's surprising how much cider is misunderstood.

Basically, cider is fermented (therefore alcoholic) apple juice. Think about the relationship between grapes and wine – the same goes for apples and cider.

Curiously though, across Britain we tend to think of cider more like beer than wine, even though beer is made from barley and hops, using an entirely different process.

Admittedly, the biggest commercial brands of beer and cider have a passing similarity, and we tend to drink them the same way – somewhere between four and five per cent alcohol, very cold, fizzy, from a bottle, can, or pint glass from a pub beer tap. If we were being unkind we might also suggest that the biggest selling brands of each are so bland they (lack) taste very similar to each other.

But cider ferments naturally to between six and eight per cent alcohol, not four or five, and in many countries it is seen as more comparable to wine than beer – in some places it's even called 'apple wine', as it was in the UK a few centuries ago.

Cider can do things both beer and wine can, so it's useful to compare it to both. But it also has some special qualities you won't find anywhere else, that make it a unique and multi-faceted drink.

So what's 'craft cider'?

There's no precise technical definition, but the word 'craft' is very useful in making an important distinction between the kind of ciders being made on a small scale and the big supermarket brands.

A typical supermarket cider is a huge commercial enterprise. It's only possible to meet that kind of scale and continuity of demand by using apple concentrate which is then watered down. The process of concentration and reconstitution destroys some of the flavour compounds that give cider its character. Reducing the alcohol content to commercial levels can make it even more tasteless, so sugar and artificial flavours, colours and aromas are often added, along with stabilisers and preservatives. Until 2010 there was no legal minimum amount of apple juice necessary before you could call something cider – now, you can legally sell 'cider' with as little as 35 per cent juice. Most commercial brands contain between 40 to 50 per cent apple juice.

The Campaign for Real Ale (CAMRA) has a definition of 'real cider' that rules out all these practices, and gives you the flat, sometimes cloudy cider many people refer to as 'Scrumpy'.

We believe that CAMRA's definition, while certainly useful, also rules out a few very good products. For example, according to them, artificial carbonation is a no-no, and sometimes we like a bit of gentle fizz in our cider. They're sniffy about filtering it to make it clear too. And while we're not huge fans of ciders with additional fruit, if people want to experiment by adding natural fruit such as strawberries or raspberries (and some do) we don't see why they should be punished. But according to CAMRA, that's not 'real' either.

We can agree on most things though, so a user-friendly definition might read as follows:

Craft cider is handmade in small batches. It only contains fresh pressed juice, not juice concentrate, and is a hundred per cent pure juice, or close to it. It has no artificial colourings, flavourings or aromas added.

Because harvests vary, the character of the cider may vary too, though blending of different apple varieties irons out most of the kinks. Most craft cider is made from specific cider apple varieties, but some also use culinary or dessert apples.

Now doesn't that sound much nicer?

Perry: cider's difficult cousin

You've probably seen '*pear ciders*' on the shelves recently. Well, the proper name for a 'cider' made with pears rather than apples is perry. And Wales has some of the best perries in the world.

But the search for the good stuff is not without its dangers.

Commercial 'pear ciders' use concentrated juice from culinary pears. But just as cider is made from specific varieties of cider apple that aren't great for eating, so a true perry is made from inedible perry pears. And in the fruit family, perry pears are the delinquent children who do not work or play well with others.

For a start, they're very difficult to grow – farmers talk resignedly of planting 'pears for your heirs' because even when they do find the right conditions and survive the various ailments that can plague them, they take a long time to yield fruit.

About that fruit...

Perry pears are small and ugly. Most varieties have a very narrow window of ripeness – sometimes as little as two days – when they go from being rock hard and unusable to squidgy and overripe and unusable. And that point arrives at different times in the season for different varieties. Even if you think you've timed it just right, you might be in for a nasty surprise because perry pears rot from the inside out.

Assuming you get some decent fruit and mill and press it, there are so many things that can go wrong that you may well end up with vinegar, or worse – some faulty perries can pull off the special trick of smelling like cow dung and nail varnish remover at the same time.

So why does anyone bother?

Because while a bad perry is one of the worst things you'll ever taste, a good one is easily one of the best drinks produced anywhere in the world.

Perry is light and delicate, often with floral aromas and citrus hints that tease your palate with a mirage of punchy fruit flavours that remain just out of reach, but close enough that you keep drinking more, and then it develops and you realise you've found something that's cidery here, like a crisp Riesling there, throwing tantalising elderflower notes on the top and then finishing with a soft tannic tingle.

Convention has it that the 'Three Counties' of Herefordshire, Worcestershire and Gloucestershire form the only region in the world where you can make a truly great perry that can perform these gustatory gymnastics. This region certainly has the terroir and microclimate that facilitate the best perry in the world. But that terroir doesn't conform neatly to the county line between Herefordshire and Monmouthshire – the dry, red sandstone that perry trees thrive on (as much as

they can be said to thrive on anything) bleeds well into South East Wales.

There are some truly wonderful Welsh perries. If you see any by Troggi, Ty Bryn or Bragdy Brodyr, make sure you try them. They'll banish memories of Babycham and Lambrini – yes, both are commercial perries – for ever.

How Craft Perry and Cider are Made

The basic principle of making perry or cider is very simple – you squeeze out the juice and ferment it. But while juice can be extracted from grapes relatively easily, it's a little tougher with the firm, hard apple.

Apples need to be broken up into a mush before the juice can be extracted, and even then it doesn't come out without a fight. So there are several steps in the process.

Milling

In the seventeenth century came the earliest form of the scratter. This device has a hopper at the top into which apples are poured. Inside they hit a set of wooden rollers and crushing cogs studded with spikes or knives, and below them a set of closely aligned stone rollers. The pulp is collected in buckets at the bottom. In the late nineteenth century, scratters became mechanised, and the principle is still used in various different forms.

Sorting

Freshly picked and gathered apples are washed to remove dirt, twigs and leaves. Any rotten ones are picked out and discarded. (A bit of bruising is OK – some people think it actually improves the flavour).

Whole apples need to be turned into a soft mush. There are various methods of doing this. The simplest is to rely on a giant mortar and pestle – a large wooden tub with a big heavy stick. It might be basic, but it was still being used in Wales in the early twentieth century.

This was succeeded by a hollowed out log filled with apples that had a stone or wooden roller run over them. And in turn that developed into the classic stone mill, one of the most evocative images in cider making. A large, circular stone trough had an upright millstone wheel stood within it, fixed to an axis that allowed it to be pulled around the trough. This could be powered manually or, more often, by horse. It's estimated that there used to be over a thousand of these in use in Wales, and they can still be seen as garden decorations or interesting design features in pubs.

Pressing

The basic principle here is similar to straining something through a muslin bag. The apple pulp – or 'pomace' – is built into a large block known as a 'cheese'. Somerset cider makers once used straw for this but in Wales they've always preferred coarse mats made of horse hair, sisal, sackcloth or, later, nylon.

The cheeses are built up into a pile, sometimes with a wooden frame to keep them in place. A flat board known as a shooter is placed across the top, and then pressure is applied to press down the board, flatten the cheese and extract all the juice.

Cider makers such as Ralph Owen at his farm in Radnor still use traditional wooden presses, manually powered, to do this. But it's much more common to see hydraulic presses doing something along similar lines today.

Fermentation

Yeast is a naturally occurring microorganism whose sole purpose in life is to eat sugar. Wherever there is fresh fruit or juice around, yeast is in the air and on all things. One of the greatest arguments for the principle of intelligent design – not to mention

a supreme being with a slightly surreal sense of humour – is that yeast converts sugar molecules into carbon dioxide and alcohol.

Yeasts come in countless strains which affect the flavour of the alcoholic drink they create in profound ways. Since Louis Pasteur first examined them (inventing the science of microbiology as he did so) drinks manufacturers have successfully isolated single strain yeasts that produce clean flavours consistently over time. Wild yeasts are much more varied, and can produce more interesting results. Sometimes in a good way, sometimes not. Opinions are mixed on whether it's best to replace them with cultivated wine or champagne yeasts, which kill off the natural yeasts, or take a chance. In Wales there are plenty of cider makers doing each.

Fermentation takes anything from a couple of weeks to a few cold, winter months. In some places it still happens in traditional wooden barrels, but is more common in industrial juice containers, or stainless steel tanks in larger operations.

The cider will then normally be 'racked' – taken off the now dead yeast and put into clean containers to clear and condition.

It will then be packed into barrels of various kinds, bottles or 'bag-in-boxes'.

© National Museum Wales

The History of Cider in Wales

Cider's origins are lost in time. We know the Romans made it on a significant scale, cultivated different styles of apple and brought some of these with them when they came to Britain. But when they left, we have no idea if cider went with them.

There is the occasional reference to cultivated apples in the first set of Welsh laws, written between 942 and 950. People could have made cider (using the old mortar and pestle method, and straining the juice through a sack) but if they did so it would only have been on a small scale, and it wasn't recorded – because not very much of anything was. Even when we get rare snippets, we're struggling because some of the early words for cider referred to 'strong drink' or were used for drinks made from all kinds of fruit. At other times cider was included in a broader definition of wine.

It's often claimed that the Normans reintroduced cider to Britain because it was well established in Normandy at the time of the invasion, but it's not quite as precise as that. Wales remained largely independent of the Normans, and even looking at the whole of Britain there is no firm documentary evidence of significant cider making until the Plantagenet period.

There are possible references to cider being made by the wealthy de Clare family in Monmouthshire in the late thirteenth century (though it's purely coincidental that the biggest-selling cider in the UK – Strongbow – was named after the nickname given to Richard de Clare).

Anyway, cider was definitely being made in Herefordshire by the fourteenth century, so it's very likely it would have spread into Wales, mainly because there was no formal border between Monmouthshire and Herefordshire at that time – in fact much of Western Herefordshire spoke Welsh at the time.

> 66 There are possible references to cider being made by the wealthy de Clare family in Monmouthshire in the late thirteenth century 99

Monmouthshire is the area that really matters in Welsh cider, and it always has. An agricultural survey in 1899 revealed that two-thirds of the entire Welsh apple crop was grown in this one county. That's because Monmouthshire shares Herefordshire's *terroir*: the same red sandstone soil, the same gently rolling hills which avoid late frosts that can kill spring blossom and with it a whole year's harvest. The Usk and Wye river valleys have perfect microclimates with just the right amount of rain and temperature variation. Much of the rest of Wales is simply too mountainous to grow apples – although that hasn't always stopped people from making cider.

By the reign of Elizabeth I, Welsh cider making was firmly established. The absolute centre was around Chepstow, which as well as having access to all the apples was also close to the village of Penallt, which was famous for producing millstones – essential for cider making on any decent scale.

At this time Welsh cider was being exported regularly to Bristol, and there are records of exports to London in 1725. In 1786, an enthusiastic Edward Davies wrote, in a poem called *Chepstow*:

No better cider does the world supply
Than grows along thy borders gentle Wye

But long-distance deliveries to London from Wales were the exception. By the seventeenth century the great houses of Herefordshire were breeding apples and inventing the first sparkling ciders and perrys – the first to use the techniques, traditions and tall, fluted glasses that would later be appropriated by champagne.

There was no similar commercialisation of large-scale cider making in Wales. Cider became the default drink across the country, and virtually every farm had its own orchard, but production at each one remained small scale, mainly for the family and workers on the farm, with a certain amount bartered or given for services rendered. The famous diary of Francis Kilvert, a clergyman who spent several years working as a vicar in Radnorshire, makes frequent grateful references to people giving him a few gallons of cider.

But much of it was drunk by itinerant farmworkers, who travelled during harvest time to work at the places that had the best pay – and the best cider. Two to four quarts a day was typical, and was seen as an important part of the overall remuneration. As well as being enjoyable, cider was an important source of clean liquid when water could not always be relied upon.

But the practice of payment in kind was frowned upon. It was common in more industrial areas for factory owners to pay their workers in tokens rather than cash, redeemable only at the company store for products at grossly inflated prices. The 'Truck Acts' of the nineteenth century outlawed this practice to protect workers from being exploited. But when the Truck Acts were extended to cover agricultural workers in 1887, it didn't go according to plan – farmworkers wanted and expected a portion of the pay to be liquid! The Report of the Royal Commission on Labour said 'they would be very reluctant to accept a cash substitute'. Legal or not, it carried on.

Not everyone was happy about it. In 1847 a report on standards of education in Brecknock complained:

The morals of this part of the country are certainly very defective, owing to the system of drinking cider etc., so prevalent here: drunkenness is the most common sin of both farmer and their servants ... in harvest time this practice is still more prevalent.

Many people agreed with the Vicar of Portskewett, when he claimed in 1872 that 'much of the crime, poverty and degradation among many of the agricultural labourers is down to them being paid in drink.'

The Baptists and Methodists had come to exert a strong moral hold over the valleys of South Wales, suggesting heaven could only be reached by those who denied earthly pleasures. Disapproval of cider drinking grew stronger, but it seemed to have little effect. It was said that as harvesters from West Wales passed through Brecknock on their way to Hereford, they left their religion there and collected it again on the way home.

Towards the end of the nineteenth century, the invention of the mechanical scratter – somewhat lighter than a heavy stone mill wheel – led to the emergence of the travelling cider mill. Not every farmer could afford to buy the expensive new equipment, so enterprising individuals took it around the farms instead, especially in Wales. A Mr C T Morris worked around forty farms in the 1920s, reckoning the average pressing to be around 350 barrels, though some were much higher.

After the First World War there were government grants for planting orchards, and Welsh cider making went from strength to strength. But at the end of World War Two, the agricultural incentives were for planting grain to feed a rationed nation. Orchards began to be neglected. The travelling cider mill trade dried up. Over the border in Herefordshire, cider makers like Westons and Symonds – and particularly Bulmers – were growing rapidly and offering cheap, ready-made cider for anyone who wanted to drink it.

But fewer people did – the mechanisation of the harvesting process after 1945 put an end to the travelling harvest worker. Britain urbanised. And if cider is the drink of the countryside, the drink of towns and cities is beer.

In most parts of the UK, cider production ceased as a local activity and became concentrated in the hands of fewer, bigger manufacturers. As Bulmers of Herefordshire grew into the biggest cider maker the world has ever seen, any farmer who was still interested in apples as a cash crop would simply sell to them.

By the mid-1980s local history books and articles were writing about Welsh cider in the past tense. It was a dead industry. The 1987 edition of CAMRA's *Good Cider Guide* didn't contain a single entry for Wales.

But no sooner had the decline become complete than the revival began.

Inspired by the memory of his grandfather and tales of the old farm cider makers, Ralph Owen began making cider in 1976, and ten years later moved to his own farm in Radnor and began reviving the neglected orchard he found there. In 1995 hospital pathologist Mike Penney opened the Troggi Cider House in Earlswood, Monmouthshire, after the equipment he and other hobbyist cider makers had been using at Usk College since 1984 became unserviceable.

Cider had slumped in popularity nationwide, and the price being offered by Bulmers for apples plummeted. Here and there, a new generation of farmers decided to give it a try themselves once more. And maybe a resurgent sense of Welsh identity played its part too.

In 2000-2001 Gwynt Y Ddraig, Seidr Dai (a great cider maker recently relocated to England) and the Clytha Arms near Abergavenny all opened up shop. By 2003 there were enough interested parties that Dave Matthews and Alan Golding of Seidr Dai founded the Welsh Perry and Cider Society.

Success came quickly: soon Welsh ciders were sweeping the boards of prizes at UK cider competitions and festivals.

And then, the Magners Effect hit. Whatever your views on fizzy cider poured into a pint glass full of ice, the new commercial brand repositioned cider and made it interesting to a whole new generation. Cider became fashionable, and the ripples of this were felt from the biggest brands to the smallest farmhouse cider maker.

Today there are over 40 cider makers in Wales, and the principality ranks alongside the West Country and Herefordshire as one of the three key cider-making regions in the UK. True to tradition, many producers are small, supplying just a few local pubs or supplying the increasing number of festivals to have their products judged against their peers.

And most people seem happy for it to stay that way. Cider making finds itself at the heart of an artisanal Welsh food and drink revolution, with pubs and restaurants, farms and other small-scale producers all helping make this beautiful region a top food and drink destination.

ST TEILO AND APPLES

Can the Welsh lay claim to producing a Patron Saint of Apples? Very possibly. He may even have taught Brittany – today one of France's two great cider producing regions – a thing or two about apple cultivation.

St Teilo was born around AD500, the grandson of King Ceredig of Ceredigion, and was allegedly friends with and cousin to the Patron Saint of Wales, St David.

In 549 a plague swept through Wales and Teilo took the survivors from his community to Dol in Brittany, to spend time with his friend St Samson, one of Brittany's seven founder saints. While Teilo was there, he and Samson planted extensive orchards between Dol and Cal, which survive today and are still known as the groves of Teilo and Samson – and sit within a popular cider making region. St Teilo is still regarded as the patron saint of apple trees in the nearby parish of Landaul.

Of course, we will never know if St Teilo was growing cider apples and teaching the Bretons how to make cider, and we have to take into account the inclusion in his legend of tame stags carrying wood from the forests for him, an episode where he fought a dragon and chained it to a rock in the sea, and the extraordinary event after his death where three different churches claimed his body, which miraculously cloned itself overnight into three identical corpses so each church could have one.

But the story about the orchards seems to have a little more circumstantial evidence around it. If true, it at least shows apple cultivation was thriving in Wales 200 years after the last Roman garrisons left Britain, and another eight hundred years before the first documentary evidence of cider making.

© National Museum Wales

17

Cider Styles

Like wine, you tend to see cider classified as sweet, medium or dry. That's fine so far as it goes, but it doesn't really begin to describe the full range and variety cider has to offer. Here are the key dimensions of it.

The cider flavour profile

Most ciders will have a degree of sweetness. The sugars in the fruit ferment and turn to alcohol, and a few ciders are fully fermented with no residual sweetness left, and can be astringent to the point of chalky dryness. But sweetness isn't just about sugar content; it's about flavour, and even a well-fermented cider may have strong notes of fruit, or even honey or vanilla.

Then, while dryness could be about the absence of sugar, it might also come from the presence of tannin, the dry, puckering compound you get in tea, red wine – and cider apples. This gives more than one way in which you might get a balance of sweetness and dryness.

Finally, like white wine, cider is often a balance between sweetness and acidity. Acid might present itself as citrusy, tart, sourness or vinegariness. So there are three main flavour dimensions for cider, not two. And a given cider may be high or low in all three.

There may then be secondary flavours, imparted primarily by the yeast and the ageing process. Some ciders have funky farmyard notes or hints of cheese. Others may have an oaky note, or there may be strong caramel or buttery hints.

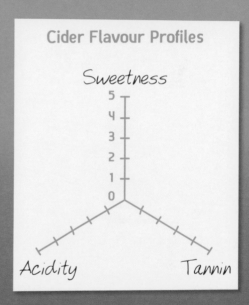

How do you like them apples?

Cider can be made from all kinds of apples – different varieties produce a surprisingly broad range of different flavours.

Eating and cooking apples

These can make perfectly good cider – or very bland cider. The relative absence of tannin in eating and culinary apples means ciders made exclusively with them become a more straightforward balance of sweetness and acidity. The bad stuff just tastes bland or excessively sweet. The good stuff compares favourably to a crisp white wine. Ciders from the eastern counties of England are often made with culinary and eating apples, and they are used by cider makers across the UK as part of a blend with other styles to boost acidity and help fermentation.

Cider apples

Far more complex and varied, and grown predominantly in Somerset, Devon and Cornwall, Herefordshire, Worcestershire and Gloucestershire, and over the border in Monmouthshire. For various reasons to do with the cultivation of apples and how they reproduce, and the most common uses to which apples were put, historically the vast majority of orchards in these areas were full of cider apples.

Any apple has a good basis of sweetness, even if the sugar will later be fermented out. Some varieties are higher in acidity than others and are referred to as 'sharp', while varieties that are high in tannin are called 'bitter'.

For the last century, the following matrix has therefore been used to classify cider apples:

Cider Apple Varieties

	Low Acid (below 0.45%)	High Acid (above 0.45%)
High tannin (above 0.2%)	Bittersweet	Bittersharp
Low tannin (below 0.2%)	Sweet	Sharp

Most ciders will be made by blending a variety of these different apples to get a pleasing end result. This might be done as the apples are going to be pressed, or after fermentation, with sharp, sweet and tannic ciders being blended together, or even both.

Talk to any good cider maker and they'll tell you at least one of two things: first, that great cider is all about great fruit, and allowing the character of that fruit to shine through. And secondly, that basic cider pretty much makes itself – it's the blending where the cider makers really get to show off their art.

Check out that body!

We really do taste with all five senses, and a lot of what we usually lump in with 'flavour' is actually mouthfeel, something experienced by your nerve endings rather than taste buds. Here again cider offers a lot of variety.

Good craft cider can be both. Some people have a definite aversion to one or the other, but we enjoy both. A cloudy, still, freshly poured pint is cider at its most natural, unfiltered and unmodified, and is usually going to feel thicker on your tongue and probably offer more complex and multi-layered flavours. But most ciders, given time, will fall clear as they age, offering something lighter and more refreshing.

In its natural state, fully fermented cider is flat and some advocates of 'real cider' argue that's the only way to drink it. But the 'naturally sparkling' method used to create champagne and some English and Belgian 'bottle conditioned' beer styles was originally devised by Herefordshire cider and perry makers, almost a century before the French 'invented' champagne. Bottle conditioned cider involves adding a dosage of sugar and yeast at the bottling stage, creating a secondary fermentation that adds natural fizz. The full process is time-consuming and laborious, so many manufacturers 'force carbonate' instead, artificially adding CO_2. While not natural and dismissed as 'industrial fizz' by some, the carbonation level can be precisely controlled to produce anything from a cola-like fizz to a gentle, soft prickle.

How about a glass of...

We'd need a book a good deal longer than this to try to create an all-encompassing classification into which every cider could fit, with each drink in just one defined category. And we believe any attempt to write that book would send us mad, which is why no one has yet done it.

But from everything we've talked about before, we can pick out a few examples to illustrate cider's range:

Bottle-conditioned cider

Usually served in strong, 750ml champagne style bottles topped with cork and wire, a bottle conditioned cider or particularly a perry can rival the French version in its clean elegance and structure.

Single variety or 'vintage'

For most of us, the word 'vintage' refers to a drink from a particular year. But it also means a drink of particularly high quality. Here, it refers to ciders made with the rare single apple varieties that produce a wonderful drink all on their own, without having to be blended with others. The Kingston Black apple has a perfect balance of sweetness, acidity and tannin – a truly great all rounder. The Dabinett is another one, medium sweet with a delicious natural spiciness.

'Keeved' cider

Keeving is a process whereby fermentation can be stopped to leave a lot of natural sweetness in the cider, getting to an alcohol range of between three and five per cent without having to add water or other adjuncts. It used to be widespread in England but is now more common in France, where it produces the characteristic French-style sparkling cider. But an increasing number of British producers are experimenting with it, including Blaengawney Cider in South Wales.

'Scrumpy'

We could all probably describe scrumpy, using a mix of language from complimentary to openly hostile. But there is no real definition of the word. It tends to refer to a still, cloudy cider, naturally fermented to around six or seven per cent, unfiltered and unpasteurised. A good one is a superb drink quite unlike anything else, but the 'farmyard' funky elements it often contains put some people off – occasionally with good reason! There is a school of thought that 'there is no such thing as bad cider,' and in darkest Somerset there are drinkers who will tell you 'the rougher the better'. But we prefer our cider free of faults and off-flavours. There's no reason that can't apply to traditional scrumpy or 'farmhouse cider'.

23

Welsh Apple and Pear Varieties

The humble apple is a truly amazing thing. It is the most mythologized and revered fruit in history. Druids used to worship the apple tree as sacred. We talk about the apple as the 'forbidden fruit' of the Garden of Eden (even though the Bible never specifies what the fruit was, and it was more likely to have been a pomegranate). And throughout our culture it's a symbol of health and happiness.

But the most amazing thing about the apple is its genetic make-up. Every apple has five petal-shaped seed chambers, with multiple seeds, and an apple tree can have over a hundred fruits. And every single one of those seeds has a different genetic make-up. If all the seeds from one apple tree were planted and carefully nurtured, the resulting orchard would probably have no two trees the same. Any similarity to the parent tree among its children would be entirely coincidental.

It's all about survival. In evolutionary terms, fruit wants to be eaten by animals who then carry its seeds away from the tree and excrete them somewhere else. In this way the trees spread. When the seeds encounter a different climate, or different soil types, some seeds are going to find it unsuitable and die, while others, completely different, will thrive.

When we find an apple variety that we really like, we reproduce it by effectively cloning it – taking a cutting from a parent tree, and grafting it onto the rootstock of another. As it grows, the resulting tree will take on the characteristics of the cutting rather than the root. The Chinese were doing this thousands of years ago, and the ancient Greeks and Romans mastered it in Europe. Ever since, any variety of apple that is known, named and understood, be it crisp Golden Delicious or a classic cider variety such as Kingston Black, began as a random seedling that someone decided had value, and then grafted.

All this means that wherever apples grow, there are varieties unique to that region – or at least, there used to be. The twentieth century saw a huge standardisation of apple varieties, with the popular supermarket ones being grafted ever more widely while quirky individual varieties were forgotten.

Welsh cider and perry are not made exclusively with native Welsh varieties, but as part of the explosion of interest in cider, those varieties are being rediscovered and propagated. The Welsh Perry and Cider Society has identified a handful of Welsh cider varieties which can be traced back to individual farms where they were first discovered and cultivated.

Breakwells Seedling is a popular variety, sharp and fruity with low tannin. Others, such as Pig Aderyn from Pembrokeshire, are rarer. There are around ten Welsh perry pears currently identified by the society, with some perry makers building an entire business around the rescue and propagation of varieties such as the potato pear. With museum orchards being planted in various places, the race is on to popularise these varieties and add to the uniqueness of Welsh cider.

> 66 The Welsh Perry and Cider Society has identified a handful of Welsh cider varieties which can be traced back to individual farms where they were first discovered and cultivated. 99

How to Drink Perry and Cider

Do we really need to be told how to drink? Surely you just pour and swallow?

Well, you can do that if you want, and *iechydd da* to you! But if you want to get the very best from your cider, there are a few guidelines – not rules – but hints and tips to help reveal your cider in its true glory.

Ambience

The perfect time and place to drink cider is the outdoors, when the weather's nice. Ideally with a rolling landscape before you and the sound of a babbling brook in the distance. We realise this is going to be difficult to achieve most of the time. But there is lots of new research suggesting that our environment really does affect our perception of taste so wherever you are, make yourself comfortable.

Glassware

Partly for the reasons of context above, partly because the right shaped glass helps release the aromas, and partly because the assumption that a pint glass full of ice may be the convention but is rarely the best way to present a cider, the choice of glass is important. If you're being offered some on a farm by a cider maker, it's best not to be rude so just accept whatever they serve it in. But at home, try a big wine glass. It looks nicer, and if you leave a third empty it's really going to help you get the most of the aromas.

Temperature

Cider shouldn't be ice-cold, because that masks the flavours, (which is precisely why some commercial ciders are served at that temperature). Neither should it be room temperature – the custom of serving it direct from a barrel or box behind the bar dates back to a time when our rooms were much cooler than they are now. Cider should be refreshingly cool – about six to nine degrees Celsius if you're measuring.

Look

Appearances can give us huge clues about flavour. Is it clear or cloudy? Light or dark? Either is fine in cider, but darker and cloudier ciders are likely to be fuller bodied.

Swirl and sniff

When we talk about 'flavour', we use it interchangeably with 'taste.' But flavour is actually a combination of taste and aroma, and the vast bulk of it is experienced in the nasal cavity. Swirl the glass to release the volatile aroma compounds, and stick your nose in. You're not expecting merely to smell apples – cider is way more complex than that. Look for big fruit aromas, including pear, melon and citrus. There may also be funky, cheesy barnyard notes, and in small doses a light vinegary hint is acceptable.

Take a glug

Have a generous sip – and keep it in your mouth. There are taste receptors all over your mouth, not just your tongue, so roll it around. Be mindful: what's happening in there? What associations does it evoke? Is it sweet or dry? Is the sweetness sugary, fruity, or reminiscent of vanilla or honey? Is the dryness crisp or chalky? What about acidity? Is it sharp, tart or sour?

Swallow

The only reason you see professional tasters spitting is that they can taste up to a hundred different drinks in one sitting. For the rest of us, you don't want to waste it! Anyway, the finish when you swallow is an important part of the overall sensation. Does it leave your palate crisp and tingling and ready for more?

Repeat

We're not (just) being facetious about this. With a good perry or cider, the flavours develop and open up the more you drink. The third or fourth sip is rarely the same as the first.

Welsh Cider Producers

There are now over forty producers making cider across Wales, and that's why this book needed to be written. While most are based in the traditional heartland of Monmouthshire, they now spread all over the country.

This guide doesn't include every single cider maker in Wales, because many are so small it wouldn't be helpful to them, or to you if you were trying to find their cider. This is a genuinely artisanal, small-scale industry, which is growing rapidly. Some producers are just making enough for their own consumption. Others are selling only to one or two local pubs, on an irregular basis. We've had to use our judgement, and exclude some who have asked not to be featured.

There's an intriguing variety among the producers, and a sense of something brand-new being built amid the ruins of a once-widespread cider culture. It all starts with the apple, and relatively few producers are lucky enough to have their own orchards. Those that do are planting and grafting trees, reviving orchards after years of neglect. Others buy their apples in, or have them donated by people who have trees growing in their gardens or on their land but have no use for the fruit. Some enterprising smaller producers even scour country lanes searching for forgotten trees, ivy-encrusted and overgrown relics by roadsides and in hedgerows and corners of fields.

The uncertainty of supply means you never quite know what you're going to get, which can be refreshing in an age of increasingly corporate conformity. But it does mean that for some cider makers listed, we can't guarantee when or where you will be able to get their products. Not everyone sells direct to the consumer, though we have listed those that do. Many produce just for festivals – and there are plenty of these listed later in the book.

So we recommend approaching Welsh cider in the spirit of a treasure hunt. This guide gives you clues, not always answers. The joy of Welsh cider for producers, stockists and drinkers alike is its sense of discovery and adventure.

The early craft beer movement in the United States used to be like this twenty years ago. Those who were there tell of a genuine sense of excitement when you found a beer you'd been looking for. These days, when many brewers have lost touch with their amateur roots and grown into sizeable factories with marketing departments and visitors' centres, many wish it could be like the old days. We urge them to come to Wales and switch to cider instead. Twenty years from now, you'll be able to say you were here when it was at its freshest and most exciting.

> 66 The uncertainty of supply means you never quite know what you're going to get, which can be refreshing in an age of increasingly corporate conformity. 99

Dee Cider ❶

Bryn Teg Holdings, Mertyn Downing Lane,
Whitford, Holywell, CH8 9EP
Contact: Scott Johnson
T: 07803 715375
E: DeeCiders@aol.com

At the time of writing, Dee Ciders is North Wales'
newest cider. Cider Maker Scott Johnson buys in
most of his apples, but he's also planted 26 different
varieties on his parents' farm (his father Richard and
friend Warren are partners in the business) to figure
out what varieties work best there. When he reaches
his conclusions, he has a 2.5-acre field ready for an
orchard to go in.

His early attempts are very promising – the cider we
tasted is sweet and full of gooseberry and berry fruit
notes, almost like a fruit cider (even though it's all
apples) but satisfyingly dry at the end.

Often available at the Blue Bell Inn, Halkyn, and does
many cider pressing demonstrations at events across
North Wales.

Visitors welcome by prior appointment during pressing
season. No farm gate sales.

Morfa Nefyn Orchards ❷

Pwll Brwyn, Lon Uchaf, Morfa Nefyn,
Pwllheli, Gwynedd, LL53 6AD
Contact: John Cooper
T: 01758 720039
E: bodger.cider@gmail.com

John and Karen Cooper began making cider as a hobby
in 2005, after being inspired by a visit to the legendary
Broome Farm in Herefordshire. Initially they scrounged
eating apples from friends and neighbours, but as their
passion grew they planted their own orchards in 2008.
They pressed their first apples in 2011, and the first
Bodgers ciders appeared the following year. They hope
to make 4-5,000 litres of cider a year, and are currently
supplying local pubs around Pwllheli.

With a deep love of all things countryside, they hope to
open up their cider farm to regular weekend visitors,
and inspire others in turn.

Visitors welcome by prior appointment.

Pant Du ❸

County Road, Pen-Y-Groes, Gwynedd, LL54 6HE
Contact: Richard and Iola Huws
T: 01286 880808
E: post@pantdu.co.uk
www.pantdu.co.uk

Pant Du vineyard was first planted in 2007, and in 2010
produced its first vintage of Pant Du wine which won a
United Kingdom Vineyards Association (UKVA) bronze
medal in 2012. As well as the vines, this
family run business also planted 2,800
apple trees, of which 2,000 are traditional
cider apple trees and the rest are Welsh
native varieties. The apples from these
trees produce Pant Du Cider, available
still and sparkling in stylish bottles.
Visitors are welcome - there's a
visitor's shop and tea room with
stunning views of Snowdon and
Caernarfon Bay, and there's even
a guided tour of the orchard and
vineyard with glass in hand.

Check website or Facebook for
opening times.

Rosie's Triple D Cider

Dafarn Dywyrch, Llandegla, Wrexham, LL11 3BA
Contact: Steve Hughes
T: 01978 790222 / 650
E: sjhddd@btinternet.com
www.rosiescider.co.uk

Between Wrexham and the harsh beauty of Denbighshire, various main roads converge, bringing tourists from Manchester, Liverpool and Yorkshire to see the sights. At one big road junction at the bottom of the Horseshoe Pass, there's a sign for Rosie's Triple D Cider, just yards away from the farm where it is made. In business, location is everything.

Steve Hughes has been making cider at the bottom of the pass since 2005. He won a gold medal at the Welsh Championships with his first ever attempt, and continued developing his hobby from there. In August 2011 the hobby became a profession when Steve quit his job in a factory and went full time.

A month later, Steve opened a cider shop on the farm, and the sign by the junction has helped make it a steady success. "We've been open just a year," he tells us when we visit in September 2012, "and the only days we haven't had customers are January 4th and last Monday." Pretty impressive for a place that looks windswept and desolate if you're just driving past.

But the farm at Llandegla ticks over steadily. Steve's dogs, kept in a fenced enclosure at the back of the yard, greet every new arrival with a volley of excited yapping, and they're rarely quiet as a steady stream of customers park up to visit the shop. One man comes in on the pretext of asking if this is the place that sells glass butterflies, or where that place might be. Once he's here, he decides he might as well try some ciders and ends up buying a range to take away.

This is a one-man business, which has its advantages as Steve is a natural salesman for his own products. In his first year he produced five gallons. Last year he did 11,500, making him the second largest cider maker in Wales. On the day of our visit a shiny new fermenter, just delivered, sits in the yard waiting to be installed. Business is growing.

As well as selling direct, Steve sells at farmers' markets and county shows, and his bottles are increasingly available in good delis, farm shops and off-licences across Wales.

Steve has won awards every year he's been in production, and it's not hard to see why. All products are 100% natural squeezed juice. Rosie's Triple D Cider (7% ABV) is full of mouthwatering fruit flavour and available in medium, sweet or dry. Wicked Wasp (7.2% ABV) is matured in whisky casks for a hint of vanilla and whisky, while Black Bart (7.2% ABV) gains a buttery nose from maturation in rum casks. There's also a very good medium perry (6% ABV) with glittering carbonation and delicate pear flavour, and an oak matured dry scrumpy (7.2% ABV) that's almost wine-like in its delicacy and structure.

Berryhill Farm Cider 5

Coedkernew, Newport, Gwent, NP10 8UD
Contact: Brian Clatworthy
T: 01633 680938

Small-scale producer who mainly supplies local beer and cider festivals. There is a farm shop, which has featured on *Rick Stein's Food Heroes*, and opens 9am to 5pm Tuesday to Saturday, 9am to 1pm Sunday.

Blaengawney Cider 6

Blaengawney Farm, Hafodyrynys,
Crumlin, NP11 5AY
Contact: Andy Hallett
T: 01495 246629
E: andy@blaengawneyfarm.co.uk
   info@halletsrealcider.co.uk
www.blaengawneycider.co.uk
www.halletsrealcider.co.uk

Andy Hallett is in the middle of apple pressing when we arrive on his farm. He greets us, resplendent in a sticky brown apron and filthy red and white polka dot welder's hat, taking just long enough out of his schedule to talk us through his cider range and indulge in some salacious gossip before getting back to sorting his apples by hand as they go into the washer, every now and then picking one out that doesn't make the grade and tossing it over his shoulder into the woodland that slopes down away from the barn.

Blaengawney Farm is 1,000 feet up at the top of a mountain with breathtaking views across the valleys. The track up to the farm can be hair raising in the wrong kind of weather, but it's worth the effort. For here is not just a farm selling two different cider brands, but also a cider barn, the headquarters of the

Welsh Perry and Cider Society, and the venue for the occasional cider festival. If that all sounds like you might not want to drive back down the track afterwards, you can hire the farmhouse for a short break.

Andy worked in engineering before he and his wife Annie decided they wanted to wind down and get out of the smoke, and bought the farm around the turn of the millennium. He began making cider a couple of years later, and what started as a hobby is now the main focus of the business. So far, he's planted 1,200 trees on the 25-acre farm.

Andy's background gives him a rare perspective on his chosen craft. In one corner of the cider barn is a small laboratory – something you don't expect to see in a business on this scale. But as an engineer, rigour and analysis is second nature. "This is where quality starts and finishes," he tells us. "I measure everything, every year, and that builds a basis for year-by-year comparison and builds your knowledge base about what's happening and how to do it well."

The rigour and seriousness with which Andy takes his product is matched by a sense of mischievous fun and playfulness which creates a perfect balance for a cider maker – someone who knows how to make a great product, and knows how best to enjoy drinking

it. We only wish we could repeat some of his jokes and observations, but there are laws about that kind of thing when it gets into print.

The cider making operation is two businesses in one: Hallets and Blaengawney. Blaengawney is traditional 'real cider' sold at real ale festivals and food fayres. Blaengawney Perry (4.2% ABV) is delicate and fine but with good fruit character. Heartbreaker (7% ABV) is Andy's favourite, bone dry as cider connoisseurs like it, but still retaining a good fruit character. Blindfold (6% ABV) is medium, with good sweet fruit, a hint of caramel and a sharp finish. National Treasure (5% ABV) is kept sweet using the ancient method of keeving, whereby fermentation is stopped before all the natural sugars in the fruit have turned to alcohol, and is like biting into a fresh apple.

Andy briefed a design agency to come up with an idea for putting his cider into bottles, and they recommended calling it Hallets Real Cider (6% ABV), which is easier to ask for in the kind of bar where stylish bottles like this are sold. It looks like a designer commercial cider, but tastes like a sparkling real cider – gently carbonated with a wonderful balance of sweetness, acidity and tannin. It will never be as big as it could be because it is still made entirely by hand.

All the ciders are multiple award winners in and out of Wales, with Andy achieving Champion Cider of Wales in 2011 and Champion Perry of Wales in 2012.

Visitors welcome if you call ahead, and cider is for sale at the farm. Blaengawney also has a fully licensed cider bar but call first in case Andy is out delivering. You can even hire the bar exclusively.

Bragdy Brodyr

7

Glynneath
Contact: Richard Williams
T: 01639 720693

Small operation that makes cider mainly for friends and family but also manages to supply a few serious cider pubs and local beer and cider festivals, where they do very well, winning regular awards. Silver Lady, a sweet perry, wins gold in its class most years at the Welsh Perry and Cider Championships.

Wholesale only, no visitors.

Clytha Perry

8

The Clytha Arms, Near Abergavenny,
Monmouthshire, NP7 9BW
Contact: Andrew Canning
T: 01873 840206
www.clytha-arms.com
E: info@clytha-arms.com

As well as running one of Wales' greatest cider pubs (see p64) Andrew Canning also makes his own perry on the premises. There are lots of indigenous perry trees in the area, some hundreds of years old. This is classic perry country, so he began collecting pears and making his own perry, originally pressing the juice through tea towels. When this worked out well he bought a small scratter and now makes three or four barrels a year. People bring unwanted perry pears from their gardens to the pub for Andrew to use. One man brings bags full of these precious jewels every year, because otherwise they lie rotting in the garden his dog eats them and throws up.

Of course, the resulting perry is very fine indeed. It is quite tannic, so he ages it for two years to mellow it. It's only sold through the pub – and only when it's ready.

Gwynt Y Ddraig

9

Llest Farm, Llantwit Fardre,
Pontypridd, RCT, CF38 2PW
T: 01443 209852
E: sales@gwyntcider.com
www.gwyntcider.com

Just like everyone else, Wales' biggest cider making business began as a hobby. In 2001 Bill George, a keen home wine maker, and his nephew Andy Gronow, scrounged together some apples at random and made an experimental first batch. It turned out that the apples had a very high sugar content, and the resulting cider came in at around 9% ABV. Friends and family, perhaps unsurprisingly, loved it and clamoured for more, but Bill and Andy realised they couldn't repeat their random mix even if they wanted to, and embarked on a more methodical approach.

Their first commercial, less potent cider shocked everyone when it won the Gold Medal at the CAMRA Champion Cider and Perry Awards in 2004 – the first Welsh cider to do so. This brought Gwynt Y Ddraig to national attention. Shortly afterwards, Magners sparked the cider boom, and demand exploded.

"Yes, Magners was a lift for everyone who makes cider," says Bill. "But that general increase in interest is not enough on its own. You still have to make a good product."

Gwynt Y Ddraig has continued to win awards, and sales are now increasing by 60% every year, so it's safe to assume Bill has no worries on that score. His farm, which has focused on cattle for three generations, is now blending, filtering and bottling cider ten hours a day, six or seven days a week.

There's a house style to Gwynt Y Ddraig's range that walks a neat balance between character and substance and broad appeal. You could never call them bland, but neither are they difficult or intimidating. "We know how we like our cider, and a lot of people agree with us," says Bill. "It's all about getting a nice, easy balance between sweetness, tannin and acidity."

The recipe changes depending on what fruit is available and the quality of the harvest, but standards never slip. All but one of the ciders is filtered for clarity, but all ciders are a hundred per cent squeezed juice with nothing else added.

The range of ciders and perrys is huge, but there are some clear favourites within it. Black Dragon (7.2% ABV), which is on the bar in J D Wetherspoon pubs across the UK, is dry and oak aged, combining strength and depth with easy drinkability. Two Trees Perry (4.5% ABV) is light and citrusy, a refreshing summer drink. Happy Daze (4.5% ABV) is a recent addition to the range, a medium, well-balanced cider that again aims to be the perfect summer evening libation.

But there's also something for those who like their cider a little more complex. Dog Dancer (6.5% ABV) is medium dry, but with a sharp, acidic edge, while new launch Tremletts Bitter (5.3% ABV) puts bittersweet cider apples to the fore with a dry, tannic edge.

There's a wide variety of bottled and draught ciders, and for any pub wishing to stock Welsh cider, Gwynt Y Ddraig tends to be the first port of call. Of all the ciders in this book, theirs is the easiest to find. But if you want to go direct, visitors are welcome by prior appointment, and there is a cider shop on the farm.

Mill House Cider

Gower Heritage Centre, Park Mill, Gower, SA3 2EH
T: 01792 371206
www.gowerheritagecentre.co.uk

The home of two of Wales' finest cider events (see p78 and p89) also brews some decent cider and perry of its own. There's a small orchard on site, and the ancient mobile press that gives demonstrations to visitors works perfectly. The cider is deep rusty red, 7.4% ABV, sweet and sharp. The perry is light, golden and refreshing and 5.4% ABV.

Palmers Upland Cyder

Rogerstone, Newport
Contact Name: Phill Palmer
T: 01633 876333
E: filpalmer@hotmail.com

Phill Palmer cares passionately about the difference between pure 100% juice cider and the mass-produced stuff available in Britain's pubs, which is 40% apple juice (if you're lucky) and 60% water, sugar and chemicals. So he refers to his product as 'cyder' to make a distinction between the two. Historically, 'cyder' is much more than an archaic spelling of the modern word. In Herefordshire in the seventeenth century, gentlemen farmers with large estates improved cider making methods in an attempt to create a drink that would rival French wine. Apples were stored to mature after picking, and then the first runnings of the press would be collected separately in the belief they made the finest cider, before the rest of the juice was fermented to make a cheaper product. This fine first pressing was often referred to as 'cyder', and while the two spellings went on to become interchangeable, Phill is one of several producers seeking to reclaim the term for the finest quality cider.

He sources most of his apples from Wales, and produces a wide range of ciders and perrys that have won awards in both Wales and UK competitions.

Wholesale only, no visitors or farmgate sales.

Raglan Cider Mill

Tynewydd Farm, Llanarth, Monmouthshire, NP15 2LU
Contact: Sally Perks
T: 01600 780258
E: info@raglancidermill.com
www.raglancidermill.com

When you first meet him, James Perks comes across as decidedly more English than his Welsh cider making peers. His shock of blond hair, stocky build, mustard corduroy and foxhunting horn ringtone on his mobile phone have earned him the nickname 'Boris'. As soon as you spend the slightest amount of time with him this seems unfair – he's far better company than the London mayor – but he's taken the comparison in good humour, going so far as to name one of his ciders Boris' Brainbender.

James' day job is land management, looking after various estates on behalf of their owners. Given his location in Monmouthshire, near the Herefordshire border, he kept coming across neglected apple trees. While drinking in the Clytha Arms just up the road, he was persuaded to make cider with them. Soon he was planting his own trees. Together with his wife Sally, he began making cider in 2006, and was named best newcomer at the Welsh Cider Championships in 2007.

The trees have become a passion. With the Welsh Perry and Cider Society, James has planted two of every known Welsh cider and perry variety in a museum orchard on his own farm. This hasn't been without its hiccups. When we visit, we're surprised to see a high barbed wire fence around each trunk. "I used wire mesh at first. But the rabbits just chewed through that to get to the trees." Suddenly the interest in hunting seems a little more understandable.

James focuses on picking the best quality fruit, which he sends to be contract pressed elsewhere before bringing the juice back here and fermenting and ageing it in wooden barrels in his cider barn. All his ciders are 100% juice with no added yeast, sugar or water.

The main Raglan Cider Mill product is RCM Dry (6% ABV), dark and rich with lots of fruit and a pleasing woody dryness at the end. RCM Medium (6% ABV) has more fruit against a solid backbone with good structure. Other highlights include the range of very fine perrys. Barn Owl (6% ABV) is dry and tannic and has beaten the best to win prizes at the Three Counties Show. Tawny Owl (6% ABV) is medium, and Snowy Owl (6% ABV) is sweet.

The names of the perrys were inspired by the owls living in the eaves of the old cider barn. We taste all of them – and more besides – straight from the beautiful old barrels on the ground floor of the barn. Up a flight of stairs from here is Raglan's own cider house (see p61) which makes this particular cider maker very difficult to leave.

When we finally do tear ourselves away, we're left with the impression that James Perks is a force of nature who is simply not even going to notice obstacles that might deter other people. His ciders and perrys are winning awards both in Wales and England, and we're in no doubt there's much more to come.

Three Saints Perry & Cider ⑬

Pentine Lands Farm, Llantrisant, Usk,
Monmouthshire, NP15 1LS
Contact: Jessica Deathe
T: 01291 672681

Jessica Deathe has an ancient perry orchard on her Monmouthshire sheep farm which inspired her to explore the history of perry and techniques for making a true, authentic product. She now makes a range of 100% natural juice perrys and the odd cider too.

Available from farmers' markets, the Coach & Horses in Chepstow, and directly from the farm. Laughing Juice (6% ABV) is the best seller, a medium perry. Nice Boys Medium Perry is a refreshing 3.5% ABV, and Blush Sweet Perry (4.3% ABV) is a single variety using just Welsh Blakeney Red pears.

Troggi Seidr ⑭

Lower House Cottage, Earlswood,
Monmouthshire, NP16 6RH
Contact: Mike Penney
T: 01291 650653
E: michaeldpenney@gmail.com

Mike Penney moved to Monmouthshire in 1983 and began making cider and perry the following year, making him one of the very first people to revive cider making in Wales.

At a hobbyist level it had never quite died out, and Mike was able to take advantage of a contract milling and pressing service at Usk Agricultural College. He enjoyed the results, and started to sell commercially, naming the business after a brook that borders his land. When the college press became unserviceable he moved elsewhere, and eventually bought his own equipment in 1989. In 1995, he opened a cider house on the property.

Mike specialises in whole juice dry ciders and perrys and used fruit sourced only from Monmouthshire orchards. He is especially highly regarded for his perry, which many aficionados believe to be the best in Wales. It has certainly won enough awards to justify the claim; most recently clearing up at Putley Cider & Perry Trials 2013 with Best Product in Show and Overall Champion Perry Maker.

While you're likely to see still versions at festivals, his particular speciality is sparkling perry, using the methods pioneered in Herefordshire four hundred years ago before they were appropriated by French champagne makers.

Visitors by appointment only, no farm gate sales.

Ty Bryn

Upper House Farm, Grosmont,
Monmouthshire, NP7 8LA
Contact: Tony and Jo Watkins
T: 01873 821237
E: tybryncider@btinternet.com

Ty Bryn is a working farm that has been in the Watkins family for three generations. Tony Watkins began making cider in 2003, producing 150 gallons in his first year. The business has grown steadily since then and it now complements the established sheep and beef farming on the property. Juice is pressed on the farm and matured in oak barrels in a seventeenth century stone cellar. In 2010, Tony's perry was named the Welsh Champion at the Welsh Perry and Cider Championships.

These multi-award winning bottled ciders and perrys are available from various local shops and pubs and at agricultural shows throughout the year.

Visitors welcome by prior arrangement.

Ty Gwyn

White House, Crossways, Newcastle,
Monmouthshire, NP25 5NS
Contact: Ben or Alex Culpin
T: 01600 750287
E: info@tygwyncider.co.uk
www.tygwyncider.co.uk

Ben and Alex Culpin both worked in the music business when they came down to visit their stepfather's farm, enjoying time out overlooking the stunning Monnow Valley. At that time, the farm grew cider apples for Bulmers and blackcurrants for Ribena. Alex was the bassist in Britpop band Tiny Monroe, and Ben worked in music publishing.

Ben enjoyed helping make a bit of cider, and one day realised that he enjoyed it far more than his day job back in the smoke. He's allergic to beer but discovered he had a great palate for cider, and decided he would rather do something good and wholesome than carry on in the corporate rat race.

In 2007 the two brothers launched their own cider, Ty Gwyn, with Ben making the cider and Alex looking after sales and marketing. The two-man operation works well and the business has grown quickly. While they send the usual bag-in-boxes and minikegs to festivals and pubs, most of what they make is bottled, and they now sell 45,000 bottles a year.

The bottle design is clean and contemporary and helps Ty Gwyn punch well above their weight, but it's the cider itself that wins both long-term fans and awards. There are two varieties: Ty Gwyn Medium Dry (6% ABV, with a red label) is a blend of Vilberie and Brown Snout apples that's characterful enough to engage the cider connoisseur and clean and fresh enough to offer a vastly superior alternative to mass-market brands for everyone else. But for us, the real star is the single variety Dabinett (6.5% ABV, grey label). Described as medium, it shows just how inadequate that term is. Dabinett is a famous Somerset apple variety that has all the qualities you would normally only expect to achieve by blending. This showcase of the apple is clean and simple, sweet yet dry, fruity and acidic with a dry, earthy, spicy backbone.

Ty Gwyn sell 40% of what they make direct from their farm shop, which is open to visitors most days. They also supply local pubs and restaurants and can often be found at food festivals.

Wernddu

Wernddu, Pen-Y-Clawdd, Monmouth, NP25 4BW
T: 01600 740104
E: info@wernddu.com
www.wernddu.com

Leigh and Frank Strawford are organic farmers and winemakers in the hills overlooking the Wye Valley, and also do a nice line in cider and perry. Black Dingle is a medium cider at 6% ABV. Wernddu Over the Hedge perry (5.5% ABV) is made from three ancient trees – over 120 years old – growing at the edge of the farm garden, which yield Helens Early and Potato Pears – two rapidly disappearing varieties. And if you need an excuse to visit and taste, there's also a herd of child-friendly alpacas.

They sell at food markets and festivals around South Wales. Visitors welcome by prior arrangement.

Berriew Cider & Apple Juice (18)

Argoes, Berriew, Powys
Contact: Gerald Davies
T: 01686 640291

Gerald Davies makes cider on a pig farm high on a Welshpool hillside. Stout and rugged, his massive sideburns sprout from beneath a leather cowboy hat, which he is never seen without.

"There's only one job I can't do with this hat on," he smiles.

"Oh yeah?" we laugh, expecting some risqué joke.

"And that's sheep shearing."

It wasn't our fault we expected a bad joke: as he shows us around, Gerald is shadowed constantly by a three-legged cat named Boozer, "Because it's legless."

Gerald has been making cider here for around seven years. He began pressing apples just for personal use, and then one autumn found himself with so many apples he ended up filling 400 barrels. He was already taking his home made chutneys to farmers' markets, so he started taking the cider along too. Since then he has given his cider to both the Queen and Prince Charles at different markets.

Gerald matures all his ciders in whisky and rum barrels. He only uses a barrel once, "because the quality goes after that," but he's amassed a huge collection. When we visit, he tells us that he neglected one batch and let it go a bit sharp, so he's now selling it as cider vinegar. His practical, improvisational approach clearly works: it's the nicest vinegar either of us has ever tasted.

The core range consists of Berriew Dry (6% ABV), which is spicy and warming with a vanilla character and a very dry finish, and Berriew Medium (6% ABV) which has sugar added to create a pleasing toffee apple character.

Gerald doesn't sell from the farm and can't accommodate visitors, but his ciders are readily available at farmers' markets, food festivals and agricultural shows.

BERRIEW
Maldwyn Medium
CIDER
Traditionally made by a man who knows his apples!
ARGOED, BERRIEW, POWYS SY21 8QG. Tel: 01686 640 291
750mL PASTEURISED CIDER. ALCOHOL 6% Vol.   BEST BEFORE: SEE BASE

Old Monty Cider

19

Glascoed, Garthmyl, Montgomery, SY15 6RT
Contact: John Jenkins
T: 01686 640899
www.oldmonty.co.uk

John Jenkins has been making cider for over twenty years, but in 2007 he started taking it more seriously. He cut the day job down to three days a week and began selling at more shows and festivals. "It's very easy to let this drift from being a hobby to a commercial business," he says, "but the trouble with being small is that I still miss a lot of the festivals because they happen when I'm busy collecting the apples and pressing."

John's cider making operation is a case study in just how easy that transition from hobby to career can be. He bought an old press for £200, which now sits on a patio in his pretty garden. Beside it is a garden shed that has been insulated and is kept to ten degrees Celsius, the optimal temperature for fermentation in the 50-gallon former orange juice containers he has lined up inside. With this simple set-up, he and his wife make 650 gallons a year.

Up to now John has foraged for apples locally. "There are over fifty orchards I can collect from," he says.

"A few of them are ancient, with varieties no one knows. The big producers simply aren't interested in them." In a few of these forgotten places John has replanted trees to keep them going. Throughout our conversation there's a recurring love of nature that is given perfect expression in his cider making.

But John Jenkins is also ambitious: he has won various medals and currently sells as much cider as he can make. Worried about keeping stock for local festivals, he recently bought a two-acre field in which he has planted 87 varieties of apple and 27 different perry pear varieties. In a few years he won't have to forage in abandoned orchards any more. But something tells you he still will.

The core Old Monty varieties are Rum Cask (6.5% ABV), which is medium with a fresh apple aroma, smoky hints and a touch of sharpness which begs to go with food, and a single variety Kingston Black (6.3% ABV), which is sharper and brighter with vivid citrus acidity.

Apart from the festivals, they're usually on at the Dragon Hotel in Montgomery.

No visitors at the moment but this will change when the orchard reaches fruition.

Ralph's Cider & Perry

Old Badland, New Radnor, Powys, LD8 2TG
Contact: James or Ralph Owen
T: 01544 350304
E: james@ralphscider.co.uk
www.ralphscider.co.uk

What can we tell you about Ralph? Not as much as we'd like, because he wouldn't see us.

Ralph was probably the first person to revive cider making again in Wales, having begun in 1976. And he remains one of the best, winning shelves full of awards every year. Ralph can be seen giving cider making demonstrations at various events around Wales using his ancient wood and straw press. We had to include him anyway, because it would be wrong to write a book about Welsh perry and cider without him in it.

Seidr O Sir

Bettws Cottage, Hundred House, Powys
Contact: Trefor Powell
T: 01982 570404
E: bettwscastle@yahoo.co.uk

Trefor Powell moved to this idyllic cottage in the late nineties after a career in the army. His property slopes down a steep, forested bankside to a chuckling river, and is criss-crossed with paths, little viewing areas and places to relax.

There is also a surprising number of apple trees. Trefor had always enjoyed the story of Johnny Appleseed, the American folk hero who planted cider apple trees on the wild frontier. His friends owned a cider apple orchard where the apples were going to rot, so he decided to collect them and have a go at making cider. He was only planning on making one barrel, but ended up with ten. He decided to jump in with both feet, bought a press from Herefordshire cider maker Tom Oliver, and planted his own trees.

The learning curve was rapid. He made his first cider in 2000, the year of a very harsh winter. He could see no evidence of any fermentation happening, but was forced to open it in May 2001 for the first Welsh Perry and Cider Festival. It turned out to be the best cider he has ever made, unable to be repeated.

"This is the problem when you ferment entirely naturally," he says. *"It's one hundred per cent juice, but who knows what yeast is fermenting in there?"*

One thing he can and does do is add a dose of the juice of wild crab apples, which gives his cider a characteristic sharpness. The cider we taste is Lucozade-orange with a slightly funky aroma, sharp acidity with a hint of tropical fruit and a very dry tannic finish. He may still be striving to recreate that first batch, but in subsequent years he's won a good haul of medals.

Seidr O Sir (Welsh County Cider) cannot do farm gate sales because the lane leading to the property is too narrow to meet the conditions of the licence, so unfortunately Trefor can't host visitors. But he sells wholesale and is often on in local pubs such as the Fountain in Builth Wells.

Skyborry

Lower Skyborry Cottage, Knighton,
Powys, LD7 1TW
Contact: Adam Davies
T: 07792 590367
E: info@skyborrycider.co.uk
www.skyborrycider.co.uk

Brothers Adam and Dan Davies moved back home from the city in their late twenties in search of a slower, more meaningful life. Both work outside – Adam as an organic vegetable grower and Dan as a gardener – and both are big fans of both real ale and craft cider. Combining their skills with their interests, they eventually gravitated to the latter as a career choice.

"I'm more attracted to the mysteries of cider and perry," says Adam, *"the majestic orchards and the strong annual rhythms that run through it all."*

Straddling the border, they currently source the best fruit they can from both Wales and England. In 2012, their first year of production, they made around 200 gallons of perry and 660 gallons of cider, which they have sold at beer festivals, local pubs and through a wholesaler.

The cider bug has clearly bitten hard: not wasting any time, the boys have planted an orchard in a field that belonged to their grandfather, containing a large mix of varieties including every known Welsh perry pear tree.

Visitors only by prior arrangement

Toloja Orchards

Lampeter, Ceredigion
Contact: Nikki or Kevin Sweet
T: 01570 471295
E: sales@welshcider.com
www.welshcider.com

Nikki and Kevin Sweet decided to up sticks and move to the country after tiring of the rat race, and after a false start or two they found their perfect home on a smallholding overlooking Cardigan Bay. They launched Toloja (an acronym of the names of their three children) in 2005 as a fully comprehensive business producing cider, fresh apple juice, cider brandy and cider vinegar (as well as a very popular range of mustards and preserves.) Nikki and Kevin use only Welsh apple varieties, and have planted a museum orchard to help preserve and propagate them.

Drunk Dewi (6% ABV) is the star of the cider range, a medium sweet cider that has won multiple awards. But there are many more to choose from, available direct via the website or from farm shops and food events across Wales.

Welsh Mountain Cider

Prospect Orchard, Newchapel,
Llanidloes, Powys, SY18 6JY
Contact: Bill Bleasdale and Chava Richman
T: 07790 071729 / 01686 411277
E: info@welshmountaincider.co.uk
www.welshmountaincider.com

24

Chava Richman and Bill Bleasdale are hoping to create a visitors' centre at their cider farm. We're sure it will be great, and when it opens we urge you to go. But when you do, please wrap up warm: it's 1,200 feet above sea level; on the day of our visit the wind whips across the mountain tops and scythes through you like you aren't there.

Bill and Chava don't seem to mind it as much: but then they are wrapped in several woolly layers, including hats.

Bill started his cider making business with friends eight or nine years ago, but gradually they dropped out. Then Chava, who hails from California wine country, appeared on the scene and together this couple created a single-minded cider aesthetic.

"We just use the apple juice with its own indigenous yeasts," says Bill. "This is a live, natural product, with nothing added. If you use sulphites and champagne yeasts, which are stronger than the wild natural yeasts and kill them off, everything tastes the same. You lose the funk."

This does mean that everything changes from year to year, depending on the conditions and the harvest they create. In 2011, the warmer than average temperatures increased the sugar content in the fruit and meant all the ciders fermented to around 8.5%. "They can go as high as 10% with these wild yeasts," says Bill.

It also means that blending is key. While some other cider makers like to explore the possibility of single varieties, for Bill and Chava it's all about mixing, using the full range of flavours nature places in front of them.

Bill and Chava currently source many of their apples from Craven Arms, just over the border in Shropshire. But they planted an orchard here six years ago which is starting to bear fruit. They hope to encourage more orchards in the area, and even have a nursery on site, selling hundreds of varieties of apple and pear trees.

They currently produce over 1,500 gallons a year and sell everything they make. They enjoy selling direct to the customer, and do so at farmers' markets and food fayres. They're also in a few decent food shops, but cannot yet sell at the farm gate because they don't have a licensed building.

That should come soon, in the shape of the visitors' centre. There are big plans and ambitions here, including a new cellar for ageing vintage ciders.

The total devotion to doing things naturally does mean products vary. Those we taste are complex and rich, some barrel aged, some taking their funky character from the wild yeast fermentation.

Cider makers rarely agree about much. There are those who argue vehemently against this natural approach, believing the risk of off-flavours is too great. Bill counters that a more scientific approach using cultivated yeast produces 'micro-industrial' cider with no character.

In our experience, there are good and bad examples of both. But one thing is certain: Welsh cider is more interesting with people like Bill and Chava in it.

Coles Family Brewery

White Hart Inn, Llanddarog, Carmarthen, SA32 8NT
Contact: Cain or Marcus Coles
T: 01267 275395
E: bestpubinwales@btconnect.com
www.bestpubinwales.co.uk

The Coles Family Brewery has recently outgrown the family pub (p70) which seems to be the focus of an ever-expanding, cleverly run business empire. In 2011 the Coles also began making cider, producing 200 litres which disappeared over the bar within a couple of weeks. The business quickly expanded and now makes six different ciders from a mix of apples and pears, including a couple of bottle conditioned *champenoise* varieties. Carmarthen Gold (5% ABV) is clear and sparkling, as clean and refreshing as a commercial cider but with much bigger flavour. All products are available in the pub, and there are plans to open a visitors' centre and offer tours and tutored tastings. Currently the only cider maker in Carmarthenshire, the energy and ambition here is big enough to fill the whole county.

Gethin's Cyder

33 Coronation Avenue, Haverfordwest,
Pembrokeshire, SA61 2RG
Contact: Gethin ap Dafydd
T: 07810 581554
E: gapd@hotmail.co.uk

Gethin ap Dafydd began making cider as a hobby in 2002, producing a single gallon of juice from crab apples using a domestic juice extractor. He called it *Sudd Cwmpo Drosto*, which is Welsh for 'falling over juice'. In 2003 he increased his output to twenty gallons. He began by using culinary and dessert apples because of a complete lack of cider apples in West Wales, and then started to source these from Monmouthshire. By 2004 he was up to 200 gallons. In 2007 he merged with the Abbey Apple Cooperative and *Sudd Cwmpo Drosto* became Gethin's Cider. The following year he won a silver medal at the Welsh Perry and Cider Championships.

Gethin and his partner Julie are exploring a wide range of cider making techniques. They use the *méthode champenoise* to create naturally sparkling bottle conditioned products, and the ancient method of keeving to create ciders that retain a natural sweetness without adding extra sugar.

Their dedicated and careful approach has paid off in style: in 2012 they swept the board at the Welsh Perry and Cider Championships, winning a silver medal for Sych dry cider, silver for Hapus medium and gold for Tri Cymro medium, which then went on to be named overall Welsh Champion Cider.

Visitors are welcome by prior appointment only, but farm gate sales are not available.

Pontymeddyg Cider

Dinas Cross, Pembrokeshire
Contact: Jimmy Whitworth or Dilys Morgan
T: 01348 811247
E: pontymeddyg@hotmail.com

Ponymeddygg is a small cider maker using a blend of cider, dessert, cooking and crab apples. The approach clearly works – their Dry Cider won gold in the Welsh Championships in 2012. They only make around a hundred gallons a year, most of which gets drunk by friends and family. But occasionally, local pubs around Pemrokeshire are lucky enough to get hold of some.

No visitors or farm gate sales.

Where to Drink Great Cider and Perry in Wales

Wales contains some great pubs and restaurants that help make it a wonderful place to visit. The standard of food and the selection of locally brewed beers is soaring, making this one of the most exciting gastro-tourism destinations in the UK.

But while the availability of Welsh cider in these fine establishments is growing, it's still a little way behind beer. With one or two notable exceptions, most places don't see the need to stock a wide range of different locally produced ciders the way they do cask ales, and many pubs baulk at paying the prices the maker of a handcrafted, artisanal cider has to charge when they can buy bland, mass-produced stuff cheaper. This will improve over time. But during our research we found most places would serve one or perhaps two ciders that were made locally, and then the usual large commercial brands.

So this is a list of great pubs that serve some locally produced Welsh ciders, rather than a collection of great cider pubs. There are very few of those around anywhere in the UK – but Wales does have a few that are worth seeking out.

> 66 The standard of food and the selection of locally brewed beers is soaring, making this one of the most exciting gastro-tourism destinations in the UK 99

Blue Bell Inn

Rhosesmor Road, Halkyn, Flintshire, CH8 8DL
Contact: Steve Marquis
T: 01352 780309
E: Steve@BlueBell.uk.eu.org
www.bluebell.uk.eu.org

Increasingly you see articles about how the very concept of 'the pub' is on its deathbed, how we simply don't need them any more and how country pubs in particular are closing for good.

And then you meet a publican like Steve Marquis, in a pub like the Blue Bell Inn, and while you're there you simply can't understand what the doom mongers are talking about.

The Blue Bell Inn is more than a pub, it's a community institution. It takes each aspect of what makes pubs truly special, and magnifies it. Obviously, the range of beers and ciders is broad, and obviously they are perfectly kept. Obviously, there are events and attractions that bring people in.

But Steve, the consummate publican, goes further than that. The pub's website lists every beer, cider, perry and whisky that is on now, what's coming next, and what's arriving soon. And Steve writes detailed tasting notes for every single one. Small tasting glasses are lined up behind the bar, and Steve never tires of offering you samples of something new to try, even once you've made a choice.

There's no piped music, but if it's music you want, come on Friday night for Karaoke, Sunday afternoons for live traditional jazz or folk musicians on a Thursday evening. At quieter times there's a big pile of board games to choose from. Or you could attend one of the conversational Welsh language classes – there are laminated sheets at the bar if you fancy trying to order your drinks in Welsh.

Since the decision to open a village post office within the pub, the kitchen has been squeezed out and there's no regular food offer. But if you're here on Saturday night you can enjoy 'Cheese and Pickled Night' – everyone brings cheese, and a few people bring homemade chutneys. The pub arranges everything on plates with neat flags labelling each cheese and provides crackers.

The commitment to cider is as strong as everything else. Apart from the constant range on the bar, every October Steve holds a cider festival with up to twenty different Welsh and English varieties on tap (he helpfully distinguishes the Welsh ones linguistically, denoting them seidr and perai) and holds cider pressing demonstrations from local producers.

Apart from being a wonderful place to visit in its own right, the Blue Bell acts as a true community and regional hub. It's packed full of tourist information and Steve knows all the brewers, cider makers and other great pubs for miles around. He acts as catalyst, facilitator and mentor for both pubs and producers, passing on orders and stock, advising start-up pubs on getting their selections right, and championing local cider makers.

If you need a base of operations for a trip around the best of North Wales cider and pubs in general, there's no better place.

Tafarn y Plu

Llanystumdwy, Criccieth, Gwynedd, LL52 0SH
T: 01766 523276
E: post@tafarnyplu.com
www.tafarnyplu.com

This grade II listed inn is two hundred years old, meaning drink-hating First World War Prime Minister David Lloyd George would have been familiar with it when he was growing up directly across the road. It's only 200 yards to the Llyn coastal path, making it a popular tourist spot. The pub has won many awards for its food – some of which, such as the slow roasted belly of pork, is marinated and cooked in Welsh cider.

At any given time there are around seven ciders and perrys in stock. Five Gwynt Y Ddraig ciders are permanent, as well as Ty Gwyn's Dabinett, and Tomos Watkins' Taffy Apples. Going further afield, Normandy ciders are stocked when available.

Every autumn there's a cider pressing day for the regulars, who bring apples from their gardens, throw them all in and hope for the best. The resulting cider – good, bad or indifferent – is usually drunk on the Sunday nearest to St David's Day, following a good bracing two-hour walk that ends at the pub.

The Bridge End Inn

Bridge Street, Ruabon, Wrexham, LL14 6DA
T: 01978 810 881
www.mcgivernales.co.uk

This perfect little pub, nestled in a hollow by the Ruabon Bridge over the River Eitha, was named best pub in the UK by CAMRA in 2011, and it's not hard to see why. It's the kind of place that pulls you in and doesn't let you go, with low beamed ceilings, a wood fire and the atmosphere of a decadent front room in someone's (very nice) house rather than a commercial establishment. Piles of board games and old books and magazines add to the relaxed welcome. Food is simple rolls and pork pies made with meat from butchers less than five miles away.

The stars on the bar are of course the real ales, but any pub that takes its ale this seriously is also bound to have respect for good cider. There are bottles in the fridge, two bag-in-boxes behind the bar and a handpump on it. While the selection is not exclusively Welsh, it's always good.

The Golden Lion

Llangynhafal, Denbigh, Clwyd, LL16 4LN

T: 01824 790451

E: info@thegoldenlioninn.com

www.thegoldenlioninn.com

This gorgeous seventeenth century inn is in the middle of an Area of Outstanding Natural Beauty in the foothills of the Clwydian hills, just half a mile away from the Offa's Dyke path, and offers accommodation as well as food and drink. Rosie's Triple D ciders are usually stocked, and there's an annual real ale and cider festival in July.

The Penrhyn Arms

Pendre Rd, Penrhynside, Llandudno, Conwy, LL30 3BY

T: 07780 678927

E: johnsumbland@thepenrhynarms.com

www.penrhynarms.com

The Penrhyn Arms has been named best cider pub in its region six years in a row and has been a runner up as CAMRA's National Cider Pub of the Year, and it's not hard to see why. There are over a dozen real ciders or perrys available at any time, and these are all sourced from Welsh producers. Local hero Rosie's Triple D dominates, with their full range of ciders available, as well as selections from Gwynt Y Ddraig. You can even rent an apartment above the pub (which, charmingly, the website informs you is 'soundproofed'!), if you fancy settling in to sample the full range.

The Raven Inn

Ffordd Rhiw Ial, Llanarmon-yn-Ial, Denbighshire, CH7 4QE

T: 01824 780833

E: ravenmad@raveninn.co.uk

www.raveninn.co.uk

The Raven Inn is a community run pub in the foothills of the Clwydian hills, with a reputation for great locally sourced food, real ale and cider. It's in a designated 'Area of Outstanding Natural Beauty', and is just a short walk from Offa's Dyke.

Built in 1772, it's been a community pub for centuries, but closed in 2009 when it was put up for sale and didn't reach the reserve price at auction. The community eventually succeeded in forming a cooperative to buy and run the pub, and it is now the hub of the village once again.

You can toast this heartwarming story of renewal and community spirit with pints of Rosie's Triple D and Black Bart which are both usually available on the bar.

Bunch of Grapes

Ynysyngharad Road, Pontypridd, CF37 4DA
T: 01443 402934
www.bunchofgrapes.org.uk

Owned by the immensely talented and award-winning Otley Brewery of Pontypridd, the Bunch of Grapes is one of those rare pubs that makes a concerted effort to be the best at everything it does. It combines the warm, unpretentious welcome you hope to get in a community pub with a restaurant that's featured in the *Good Food Guide*. Otley's own beers are complemented by a great selection of locally brewed real ales and interesting craft beers from around the world. The wine list is six pages long. Bread freshly baked on the premises is available for sale, alongside homemade chutneys and preserves. This all means that the clientele consists of ancient locals who still feel welcome nursing their pints through the afternoon, and serious foodies who come from as far away as London to visit.

The cider selection is also a cut above the average. Two of the handpumps on the bar are devoted to locally made ciders and perrys which rotate regularly. In addition, the fridge holds half a dozen ciders from Gwynt Y Ddraig as well as permanently stocking Hallets Real Cider, made just up the road. Unsurprisingly, the Bunch was voted the region's Cider Pub of the Year in 2010.

In the way you only get with pubs that are genuinely passionate about what they do, there is a constantly busy diary of events at the pub, from beer festivals to live music and readings and tutored tastings from drinks writers. All these, plus the most recent menus and drinks lists, are kept lovingly up to date on the website.

Chapter

Market Road, Canton, Cardiff, CF5 1QE
T: 029 2030 4400
E: enquiry@chapter.org
www.chapter.org

This cool, urban, cinema, gallery and theatre space has been named 'best bar in Cardiff' by the *NME*, and Best Place to Drink in Wales by *Observer Food Monthly*, and it really is a wonderful bar. Unfortunately the cider selection fell short of the very high standards across the rest of the drinks range when we visited, but one or two Welsh ciders were available alongside the usual mass-market alcopop ciders, and we're sure the range will have improved when we visit again.

Nantyffin Cider Mill

Brecon Road, Crickhowell NP8 1SG
T: 01873 810 775
www.cidermill.co.uk

There are so many nice pubs on the road from Abergavenny to Brecon that you might unwittingly miss the best ones. Maybe this is why the Nantyffin Cider Mill is painted pale pink.

The original building was a sixteenth century cattle drovers' inn, but it became famous for producing cider in the nineteenth century, only ceasing to do so in the 1960s. The old cider press is still in place in the restaurant, and there's an old stone mill outside.

The windows around the door are plastered with recommendations from Sawdays, Michelin and the Good Pub Guide. Any guidebook worth its salt, this place is in it. Inside it's all thick stone walls, huge fireplaces and hidden nooks.

We arrive at the end of lunch service, and you can tell it's been busy. A little girl of four is helping put sugar on the homemade scones, and asks us if we would like a raisin.

The cider selection is much broader than it is in most pubs, and even though it is not faithful to Wales, the choices from Herefordshire and Somerset that accompany the Gwynt Y Ddraig are very good.

Raglan Cider Mill - Cider House

Tynewydd Farm, Llanarth, Monmouthshire, NP15 2LU
T: 01600 780258
www.raglancidermill.com/cider_house.html

Like any true cider house, the one at Raglan Cider Mill occupies a hazy grey area between ordinary pub and private room for friends. It's neither, but shares characteristics with both.

Walking up the stairs to the upper floor of James and Sally Perks' cider house, it feels like you're entering a gang hut for grown-ups. It hasn't had much done to it, but there's not much more you would want to do. A few church pews provide the seating. The walls are plain and whitewashed, and there's a wood-burning stove at one end. A bar runs down one side, serving RCM ciders (see p39) from the barrels directly below.

The whole thing was built on barter, with friends doing the electrics or plumbing in return for a bit of free cider. The staircase down to the cellar was rescued by James from a fire. The solid plank of the bar top was discovered in a wood store in Llanarth, where it had lain for 28 years, and to the regulars supping cider on the Friday night we visit, it's an old friend.

"I know where that tree came from," says one. *"Back of the lodge, huge tree it was."*

"That's right," says another. *"The crucifixion thing was on the left hand side."*

When they see us staring at this remark there's embarrassed laughter, then someone says, *"We do things the old fashioned way out here."*

The wind blows open the rickety door every few minutes, threatening a dramatic entrance. One time it's accompanied by a young couple who moved here to take up pig farming. Soon they're in animated conversation with the old locals about the potential problems this entails. *"We've been very lucky,"* says the woman thoughtfully, *"the only one who's ever been aggressive is Flopsy."*

The Cider House serves whatever RCM ciders are ready to go down below. The food consists of the occasional bowl of crisps James puts on the bar.

Everything about this place is perfect.

This is not a full-time occupation for James and Sally – it wouldn't work if it was. The Cider House is now being advertised and is open to visitors by prior arrangement, usually on Friday nights and Sunday

afternoons. They also organise a minibus for parties such as stag nights, and there is the Welsh Perry & Cider Society's wassail here in January, with a bonfire out in the farmyard.

If you just happen to chance across the Cider House as you're passing, chances are you may not be able to visit. But it's worth organising a holiday in Wales specifically just to visit a bar that's quite unlike any other.

The Anchor Inn

Chapel Hill, Tintern, Monmouthshire, NP16 6TE
T: 01291 689582
www.anchortintern.co.uk

This ancient inn was originally built in the twelfth century as a grain store and cider mill for nearby Tintern Abbey. The old stone cider mill is a centrepiece of the main bar, and in-keeping with its origins the pub offers a decent range of local and national ciders.

The Bell at Caerleon

Bulmore Road, Caerleon, NP18 1QQ
T: 01633 420613
E: thebellinn@hotmail.co.uk
www.thebellatcaerleon.co.uk

This 400 year-old coaching inn just outside Newport was named CAMRA's Cider Pub of the Year for Mid and South Wales in 2011. It's one of those pubs that has everything: beautiful old rooms, a well respected restaurant, a great wine list and a superb range of beers and ciders. There's an ever-changing list of over twenty ciders and perrys on draught and in bottle, surely the largest in Wales. Gwynt Y Ddraig, Hallets and Raglan Cider Mill – all local to the pub – are firm favourites. The staff are so passionate and knowledgeable they can even offer advice about pairing ciders with the excellent food. Cider is also used extensively and mouthwaterngly throughout the menu - the cider-infused Scotch egg is amazing. If that's not enough, there's an annual real ale and cider festival when the range grows even bigger (dates change – but there's an events section on the website).

The Bell at Skenfrith

Skenfrith, Monmouthshire, NP7 8UH
T: 01600 750 235
www.skenfrith.co.uk

With a tiny humpbacked bridge over a small brook beneath on the road outside, a castle across the field and low, green hills all around, the setting for the Bell is so idyllic it might fool you into thinking you've wandered into an Enid Blyton storybook.

The pub itself fits well into this perfect tableau: outside there are rolling gardens with shady trees, a kitchen garden that provides much of the produce on the menu, and an enclosure with a few pigs.

The Bell is all about the championing of local produce. Rarely and commendably, this extends to the drinks range as well as the food. All beers and ciders are from Wales or just across the border in Herefordshire. Bottles of Ty Gwyn's two excellent ciders are always in stock – their farm is just a few minutes' drive away. Springfield Cider and apple juice are also favourites.

The Clytha Arms

Clytha, Near Abergavenny, Monmouthshire, NP7 9BW
T: 01873 840206
www.clytha-arms.com

Andrew Canning has run the Clytha Arms for nearly twenty years, and in that time he has made it one of the most important cider pubs in Wales. "*I've always had a good selection of real ciders,*" he says. "*I used to get a lot of them from Herefordshire but there's no need now with so many small cider makers in Wales.*"

There's always a stack of bag-in-box ciders at one end of the bar. "*I have to keep them up there – if I put them in the cellar they make the beer go cloudy*". Gwynt Y Ddraig is stocked permanently, as are ciders from the Raglan Cider Mill just down the road. Ty Gwyn is available permanently in bottle, and there's a range of constantly rotating guests.

The attention given to cider is in part simply a reflection of the high standards Andrew maintains across his business. This is a beautifully welcoming pub with open wood fires that tempt you to settle in for days. The range of real ales, many of them locally brewed, is extensive and perfectly kept. The food is of a standard you'd expect in a seriously good restaurant. The bacon, laverbread and cockles is nothing short of addictive, and the stuffed ham cooked with cider is a perennial favourite. The walls are arrayed with Pub of the Year awards at regional and county level, as well as awards from *Period Living* and *Traditional Homes* magazine for Country Pub of the Year.

But the love of cider goes further than that too. "*Cider has always been made locally around Monmouthshire*" Andrew says. "*The local farmers never grubbed up all their orchards.*" Cider is part of the identity of the area, so it's important to Andrew that it's part of the pub's make-up too. That's why he makes his own perry (see p34) as well as elderflower champagne.

For a long time this was the venue for the Welsh Perry and Cider Festival, with up to 100 tents in the grounds some years. Now that festival has moved elsewhere, Andrew occasionally stages events of his own to celebrate cider and perry.

While all the staff at the Clytha are clearly infected by Andrew's passion, when he's in the pub he is hands on. While we chat, he's constantly jumping up to adjust the chimney fan for one of the fires, welcoming people or helping staff find something. There's a distinct family feel to the pub, and as we eat our meals, the resident dogs look soulfully into our eyes. When we finally have to leave, happy and smelling of wood smoke, we vow to return as soon as we can.

The Golden Hart

20 Cardiff Road, Newport, NP20 2ED
T: 01633 254718
info@thegoldenhart.co.uk
www.thegoldenhart.co.uk

This small city centre pub recently reopened under new
ownership and put real ale and craft cider back on the
bar for the first time in years. The small cider range is
well chosen and Welsh ciders such as Troggi are
usually available.

The Star

Old Abergavenny Road,
Mamhilad, Pontypool
NP4 0JF
T: 01495 785319

Traditional country pub with a pleasant beer garden
and an unpretentious menu which makes a point of
locally sourced food. There's a good selection of local
real ales and ciders.

65

The Stonemill

Rockfield, Monmouth, Monmouthshire, NP25 5SW
T: 01600 716273
E: bookings@thestonemill.co.uk
www.thestonemill.co.uk

Definitely more of a restaurant than a pub. One of the stone cider mills after which the place is named still dominates the central space on the main floor, and makes an inspirational view particularly from the mezzanine gallery. The other is just outside, an ornament in the owner's garden.

The website boasts of a commitment to local suppliers across every aspect of the business, and true to this, both of Ty Gwyn's excellent bottled ciders are stocked permanently (the magnificent Dabinett is listed simply as 'medium') but for some reason, so is Magners. The restaurant is excellent, and very busy, and there's also a good selection of locally brewed ales. It only needs to tweak the cider range slightly to become an unmissable destination.

The Wye Valley Hotel

Tintern, Near Chepstow,
Monmouthshire, NP16 6SQ
T: 01291 689441
www.thewyevalleyhotel.co.uk

This family-run inn in the middle of pretty Tintern is an excellent base from which to see sights such as the ruined twelfth century abbey or the River Wye. The focus of the business is the restaurant, but the bar stocks a solid range of ales and ciders on draught and in bottles. These aren't always local, but they are always good.

South Wales Off-Licences

Bacchus

Beaufort St, Crickhowell, NP8 1AD
T: 01873 812229
E: paul.lowe@live.co.uk

This independent off-licence in Crickhowell is tiny but crammed with treasure, like a boozy Aladdin's cave. Features a small but perfectly formed selection of local ales and ciders.

The Bottle Shop

4 Pen-Y-Lan Rd, Cardiff CF24 3PF
T: 029 2049 0096

Primarily an independent wine merchant, owner Dan Williams (ably assisted by local celebrity Watson the dog) also knows his stuff across pretty much any beer, cider or spirit you care to mention, keeping in close contact with local producers. The range in the shop is excellent, and Dan's knowledge is second to none. If you know what you're looking for, it's probably here. If you don't, he'll help you decide.

Arth Wine

Station Approach, Penarth, CF64 1DB
T: 029 2070 1091
www.arthwine.co.uk

Billed as 'Penarth's best kept secret', it's time we let the cat out of the bag. This independent wine shop near Cardiff specialises in organic and biodynamic wines but also stocks a good range of Welsh cider, including Hallets on draught.

67

Felin Fach Griffin

Felin Fach, Brecon, Powys, LD3 0UB

T: 01874 620111

www.felinfachgriffin.co.uk

This multi-award-winning food-led pub (the word 'gastropub' does it a disservice) is one of the top places to eat and drink in Wales. Like the rest of its drinks selection, the cider list combines local with the best of the rest of the UK, with Ty Gwyn taking its rightful place alongside outstanding ciders from Herefordshire and Somerset.

The Sportsman

17 Severn Street, Newtown, Powys, SY16 2AQ

T: 01686 623978

www.hophouseinns.co.uk/The-Sportsman/

The Sportsman is the brewery tap for the excellent, multi-award-winning Monty's Brewery, and like all great brewers, they're also fond of good cider here. The cider range peaks at six in the summer, with a mix of handpull, commercial keg products and bottles. Gwynt Y Ddraig is a permanent resident "because the quality is so reliable", but there are also occasional local guests such as Old Monty's.

Food is not available because there is no kitchen, but they're happy for you to bring in meals from the takeaways around the corner. This is typical of the open, friendly attitude at the Sportsman, a 'proper pub' that knows how to give a warm welcome.

The Star Inn

Talybont-on-Usk, Brecon, Powys, LD3 7YX

T: 01874 876635

E: anna@starinntalybont.co.uk

www.starinntalybont.co.uk

Popular canalside pub which has a great beer garden, in the middle of perfect walking country. There's a B&B offering 'rural R&R,' and *Wales on Sunday* has called it 'the best proper pub in Wales'. The cider selection is good but not always Welsh, although Gwynt Y Ddraig, Ty Gwyn and Ralph's are often available. January 2013 saw the pub hold it's first Sausage and Cider event. We hope and trust there will be many more.

Every June and October the pub hosts a beer and cider festival. What's more, they were named CAMRA Cider Pub of the Year runner up in Breconshire.

Ship and Castle

1 High St, Aberystwyth, Dyfed, SY23 1JG
T: 01970 612334
E: enquiries@shipandcastle.co.uk
www.shipandcastle.co.uk

Aberystwyth's best real ale pub also takes its cider seriously. Three ciders and one perry are on the bar at all times, with Gwynt Y Ddraig Black Dragon and Two Trees perry the staples of the range. There are two real ale festivals a year, which also include a range of guest ciders and perrys.

The Eagle Inn

Castle Street, Cardigan, SA43 3AA
T: 01239 612046
www.theeagleinncardigan.co.uk

Cosy community pub that offers good home-cooked food, regular live music and a warm welcome from staff who really care about what they do. One or two ciders are usually available.

The Queens

Church Street, New Quay, Ceredigion, SA45 9NZ
T: 01545 560650
E: thequeensnewquay@hotmail.co.uk
www.thequeensnewquay.blogspot.co.uk

This delightfully eccentric place is possibly the only pub to incorporate its own bookshop, but the pub's own blog makes for fascinating reading in its own right, with entries including records for who can eat three poppadoms or drink a pint of water through a straw the quickest. The place prides itself on its excellent food and beer range, and the cider isn't bad either. Gethin's excellent cider is in stock permanently.

White Hart

Finch Street, St Dogmaels,
Cardigan, Dyfed SA43 3EA
T: 01239 612099

Pleasant old inn with a great reputation for home
cooked food. It bills itself as a restaurant but the bar
is still welcoming for a good pint. There are always a
couple of craft ciders available.

Y Talbot

The Square, Tregaron, Ceredigion, SY25 6JL
T: 01974 298208
E: info@ytalbot.com
www.ytalbot.com

A wonderful old drover's inn which has been trading as
a pub for at least 400 years. Named Ceredigion Pub
of the Year in 2012, the restaurant is outstanding and
recently renovated rooms are also available. The wide
range of local real ales is complemented by Gwynt Y
Ddraig ciders.

White Hart Thatched Inn and Brewery

Llanddarog, Carmarthen, SA32 8NT
T: 01267 275395
E: bestpubinwales@btconnect.com
www.bestpubinwales.co.uk

When your URL is 'best pub in Wales' you're setting
yourself up for a fall, but this place makes a very good
attempt at living up to such high billing. Dating back to
1371, it was originally a drovers inn but has in recent
years welcomed travellers including Prince Charles and
Dylan Thomas. The interior is as crowded and eccentric
as you'd expect from a pub this old. There's a
brewery on site which now also makes its own
cider (see p50). Food is home cooked and
available at lunchtimes and evenings every
day of the week. There's a small farm at the
back, a children's play area, and even a farm
shop selling the family's produce. Not so much a
pub as a much bigger food and drink themed
immersive experience.

West Wales Off licences

Fire and Ice

65-66 St James Street, Narberth,
Pembrokeshire, SA67 7DB
T: 01834 861995
E: info@fireandicewales.co.uk

It may seem like an unlikely combination for a business plan, but for partners Ivan Wilson and Lynne Bayliss, the twin pillars of cider and ice cream make perfect sense. Ivan is clearly someone who follows his passions. He has over 25 years experience in the photographic industry and his camera shop is just next door. In 2010 Ivan and Lynne opened a luxury ice cream parlour which quickly became just as famous for its astonishing array of ciders and perrys. There are over fifty in stock at any time, with regular Welsh ciders including Gethin's, Hallets, Springfield, Ty Gwyn, and Rosies Triple D, as well as regular guests throughout the year. And just to prove the business idea is not as random as it might seem, they bring the two sides together in the form of alcohol infused desserts. If you've never had a cider sorbet before, it's time you got yourself to Narberth.

Find out more about their range of ciders and ices on their Facebook page.

Wright's Independent Food Emporium

Four Seasons, Cwmtwrch Farm
Nantgaredig, Carmarthenshire, SA32 7NY
T: 01267 290878
E: maryann@wrightsfood.co.uk
www.wrightsfood.co.uk

Set in a former cowshed in the heart of the Towy Valley, Wright's is a deli and cafe offering delicious, mostly local, food to eat in or take away. It stocks a range of wines, craft beers and Hallets cider is available to drink on the premises or take away.

Cider is a drink for festivals. There's something about it that's more joyful than other alcoholic drinks. It's both mellow and euphoric, chilled and joyous.

As such, it fits into festivals of every size and shape in Wales, and even creates some of its own. Whether you're partying down at a big music festival like Green Man, ticking your way through as much as you can at a beer festival or taking your taste buds on a journey at a food festival, cider is always there to make everything sweeter.

Here we've gone into detail about the festivals and rites that focus specifically on cider, but also mentioned other events where Welsh cider helps enhance proceedings.

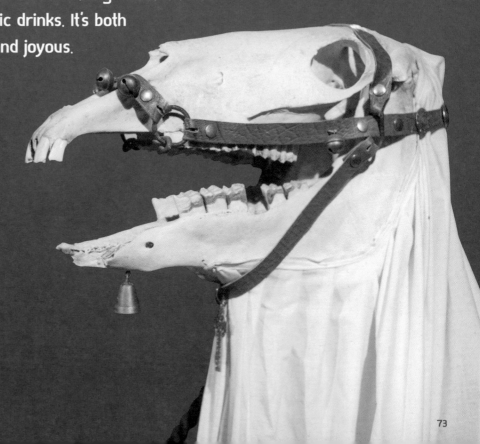

WASSAIL!

(Mid-January)
Various locations

If you haven't spent a cold January night being marched down the middle of a street following a bloke wrapped in a white blanket holding aloft a horse's skull on a stick, you haven't lived.

There are many strange customs in the world of cider, but perhaps Wassail, and its distinctly Welsh version of *Mari Lwyd*, is the oddest.

Wassail dates at least as far as the Middle Ages, and feels like a throwback to the days when druids called the shots. It is celebrated on the old Twelfth night of Christmas according to the Julian calendar – or the nearest weekend to it – and for cider, it's all about waking up the apple trees after their winter slumber. Many events take place in orchards, and no two are quite the same. They usually involve fire, lots of noise, and generous quantities of cider.

The tradition was kept alive by Morris Men, but now numbers at wassails all over the UK are surging. Sometimes the Morris Men enlist the help of a Wassail Queen. Either she or a senior Morris Man (or a druid if you have one locally available) leads the crowd in the singing of the Wassail Song. Toast is dipped in cider and placed in the branches of the trees to attract good spirits (or robins, depending on where you are). Then, a terrific noise is made either by banging pots and pans or firing shotguns into the branches of the trees, to scare away the evil spirits that prevent good fruit the following year. All this commotion supposedly also wakes up the trees, and we all think forward to renewal and new growth.

Regular wassails take place at Gethin's Cyder (page 51) and at Raglan Cider Mill (page 39).

Wassail is not exclusive to cider orchards, and in parts of South Wales it is entwined with the *Mari Lwyd* ('Grey Horse', or 'Grey Mary'). For reasons that have been lost in time, a horse's skull is fixed on top of a pole with a white sheet attached to the back, to hide the person carrying the pole. The skull may be decorated with eyes, jewels or anything else that people feel like expressing their creativity with. It is then taken from house to house – and especially from pub to pub – where its entourage sing songs at the door in the hope of being granted entry and given food and drink.

The Mari Lwyd was once popular across Wales, but for some unfathomable reason the Church began to object to this pagan revelry and it almost died out. It's now back in style, and the one in Chepstow sees Morris sides from England and Wales trade dances across the old bridge that marks the border between the country before hitting the pubs.

For all the madness, Wassail links us back to the passing of the seasons. At the bleakest time of the year, it reminds us that spring is on the way. And let's face it – there are less interesting ways of spending a wet January weekend.

GWYNT Y DDRAIG OPEN WEEKEND

(Dates vary)

Llest Farm, Llantwit Fardre, Pontypridd, RCT, CF38 2PW

www.gwyntcider.com

Each year, Wales' largest cider maker (p36-37) throws open the doors to the farm and invites you for a weekend's revelry. The modest admission fee includes your first pint or bottle of cider free, and as well as drink, there are stalls selling freshly prepared food and a programme of live music. If your interest in cider goes beyond refreshment, there are demonstrations of cider making using an old 19th century press. And if you feel like settling in for the long haul, it's possible to camp.

Dates do change and are dependent on the weather, so it's best to check the website for the latest news.

THE CIDER YEAR: BLOSSOM TIME

In late April and early May, apple blossom carpe green orchard in a blizzard of white. It's one of th most romantic times of the year, captured in poetr song, and handily, it's also when cider that has b slowly fermented and matured in the traditional manner over the winter is ready to be cracked

This makes blossom time a perfect occasion to a cider farm. The trees never look better, and th produce (from the previous year) never tastes That's why various cider-themed events and fes happen around this period. If you're in Wales fo bank holiday between Easter and June, a perfe diversion is never far away.

GOWER CHEESE AND CIDER FESTIVAL

(Mid-May)
Gower Heritage Centre, Parkmill, Gower, Swansea, SA3 2EH
www.gowerheritagecentre.co.uk

If the idea of a cheese and cider festival sounds odd, that's because you have yet to discover that cider and cheese go together like Ant and Dec – at their best, you can't tell where one ends and the other begins.

The Gower Heritage Centre positions itself as a 'vibrant crafts and rural life museum' in the beautiful Gower Peninsula. When you arrive, it's like stepping into a real world version of Hobbiton or Toytown. An eccentric

jumble of old buildings merge and tumble over each other to form a maze of narrow corridors and tempting doorways, assaulting the senses like Dorothy's first glimpse of Technicolor Oz. There's a big wooden mill wheel, an old corn mill and woollen mill, sheds painted in bright primary colours, a play area full of plastic tractors and a busy duck pond. It's an absurdly cheery looking place.

And though you will undoubtedly lose your bearings in all this, all paths eventually lead to a red-tiled courtyard surrounded by a tearoom, games arcade, puppet theatre, village shop and dairy. And for one weekend, this is the focus of the Gower Cheese and Cider Festival.

There are around twenty bag-in-box ciders and perrys available, all piled up in a wall behind one stall. Next to it is a long table featuring Welsh cheeses, soft, rich, creamy, spicy cheddars, mild and mature, some flavoured with ingredients such as mustard, chilli or beer.

Doors open late morning, and you may arrive feeling there's not enough here to sustain your interest through the day. But as you start to sample the ciders, setting up camp in the middle of the courtyard, with the kids (and some adults) entertained for hours by the toy tractor enclosure, time slips by in a suitably magical way. A stage at one end features a steady progression of musicians playing a wide variety of styles, from country and bluegrass through folk and sea shanties to pop and hard rock. Somehow, it all seems to go very well with the cider.

There's an ancient press out front that holds cider making demonstrations, and the centre's own orchard – which serves as an overspill car park – is in full blossom. With the spectacular views of Three Cliffs Bay just a twenty-minute walk away, there's also a perfect break if you want to slow things down a little.

Cider events are at their best when they feel slightly off-kilter and otherworldly, eccentric and slightly anarchic, but still somehow staying on the rails. By that standard, the Gower is hard to beat.

WELSH PERRY AND CIDER FESTIVAL

(May Spring Bank Holiday Weekend)
Caldicot Castle, Monmouthshire
www.welshcider.co.uk

The Welsh Perry and Cider Society's big annual shindig is simply not to be missed by any cider fan. A fixture at the Clytha Arms for many years, the festival has moved around a little in recent years, meaning there's always a slight reinvention of the successful basic formula of live entertainment, great food and lots of cider and perry. It has now found a new permanent home at Caldicot Castle in Monmouthshire.

There's also a serious side: this is the occasion on which the Welsh Perry and Cider Championships are judged and announced, making it the weekend every cider maker featured in this book tries to put their very best produce forward. Every year, there are between 70 and 80 different products available, showing the breadth, diversity and quality of Welsh cider and perry like nowhere else.

The event always runs over Whitsun Bank Holiday Weekend, beginning at 6pm on the Friday and running through to the Monday, which is usually a more family oriented session (noon till 6pm) with games and entertainment. If you're feeling particularly festive, camping is available for those wanting to stay for the full weekend. The website also has full details of all other accommodation options in the area.

GREAT WELSH BEER AND CIDER FESTIVAL

(Early June)
Motorpoint Arena, Mary Ann Street,
Cardiff, CF10 2EQ
www.gwbcf.org.uk

For one week in early June, Cardiff's giant exhibition and concert arena transforms into the biggest pub in Wales.

While real ale is the star attraction, organisers CAMRA are also passionate about cider, and usually have over 60 on sale, most of these from Wales.

The arena is a huge barn of a place, but unlike other events on this scale this one still retains a cheerful, festive atmosphere, thanks to live music and decent food also being available.

THE GREEN MAN FESTIVAL

(Late August)
Glanusk Estate, Black Mountains, Wales
www.greenman.net

Wales' leading music and contemporary arts festival has a more laid back, folky vibe than many music festivals around the UK and feels more welcoming, individual and interesting as a result. You don't see the same old line-up of bands, and you don't see the same old mass-market food and drink either. The most popular bar on site has a boggling array of locally made real ales and Welsh ciders, and sits in an elegant courtyard where you can pass the time between bands. You may even find one of the acts asking you to budge up to make space at the long trestle tables.

HAVERFORDWEST BEER, CIDER, PERRY AND LOCAL PRODUCE FESTIVAL

(August Bank Holiday Weekend)
E: hip.trust@tiscali.co.uk

In the beautiful setting of Haverfordwest castle, this celebration of local food and drink includes a great selection of Welsh ciders and perrys.

ST. FAGANS FOOD FESTIVAL

(Early September)
St. Fagan's Museum, Cardiff, CF5 6XB
www.museumwales.ac.uk/en/stfagans/

Showcasing the best in Welsh food and drink, from tradition and history to cutting edge cuisine, with over 80 food and drinks stalls. You will often find a Welsh cider producer with a stand here.

ABERGAVENNY FOOD FESTIVAL

(Mid-September)
Various venues, Abergavenny, Monmouthshire
www.abergavennyfoodfestival.com

Once described as the 'Glastonbury of food festivals' Abergavenny is a foodie paradise that's hard to beat, and is now one of the best events of its type anywhere in the UK.

Taking place over one weekend in September, the festival takes over the entire town. The indoor market, castle grounds and various other venues are crammed full of stalls featuring an astonishing array of food and drink. In hotels and function rooms, chefs, TV presenters and writers give talks on everything from cake decoration to foraging for your own food, and there's always a decent smattering of tutored tastings across a variety of drinks.

Welsh cider makers can be found dotted around the various exhibitors market stalls, and there's at least one beer tent that also has draught ciders available.

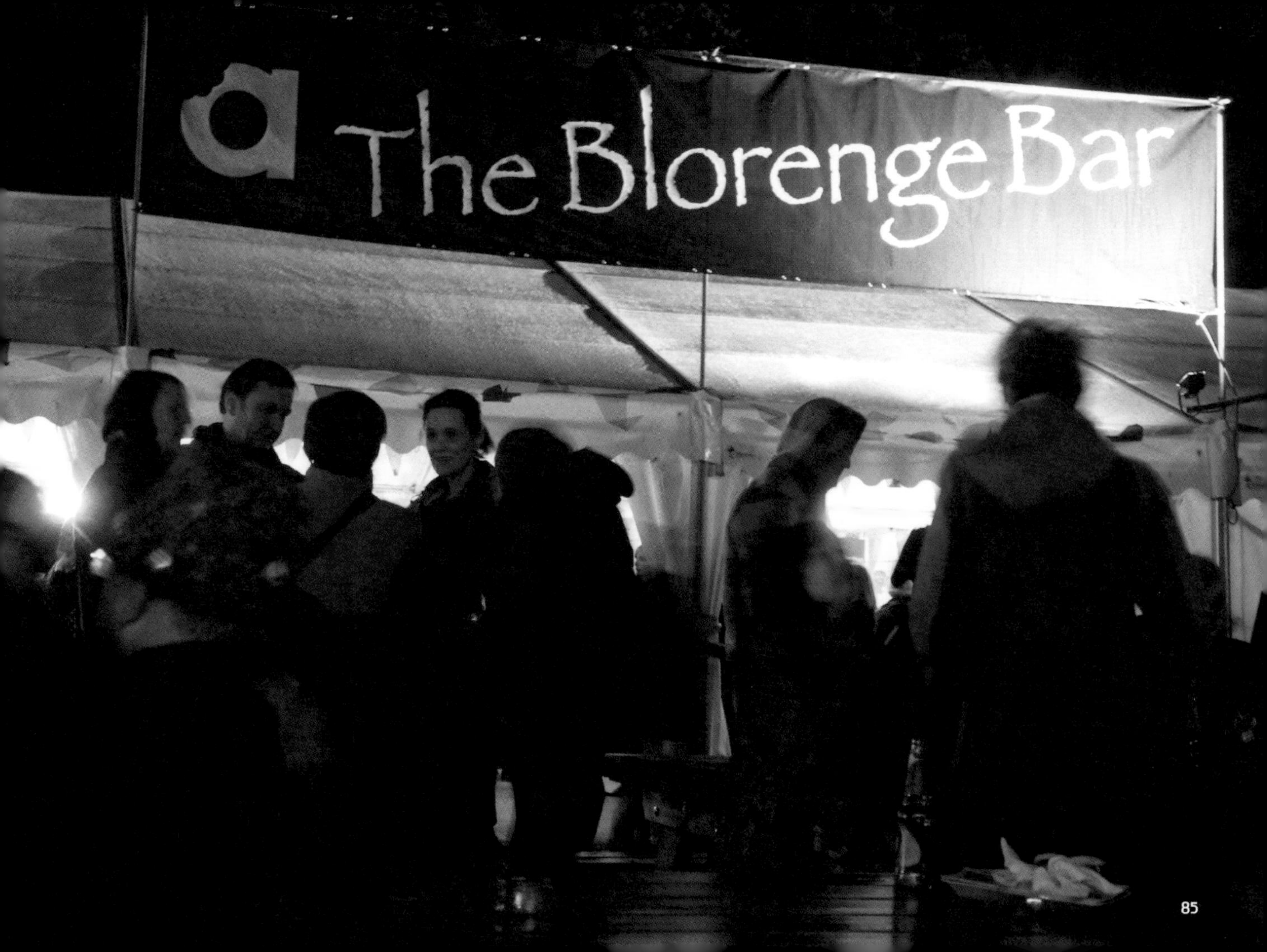
The Blorenge Bar

BRIDGEND FEASTIVAL

(September)
Bridgend
www.bridgendfeastival.com

A food festival for all the family that takes over the town of Bridgend for the weekend. A focus on promoting the best of local produce including a farmers' market, tasting tent, and food and drink stalls. A Welsh real cider tent has become a firm favourite here.

ERDDIG APPLE FESTIVAL

(Early October)
Erddig Hall, Wrexham, LL13 0YT
www.nationaltrust.org.uk/erddig/

Erddig Hall is one of those rambling, curiously ordered country estates that, if you were the National Trust, you would simply have to buy. So it's nice that they did. The beautiful 18th century house has elegant gardens sweeping away from it, and then off to one side is a maze of courtyards, orchards and walled gardens which play host to all kinds of activities. At Apple Day, as well as watching basket weaving demonstrations, buying tea towels and eating cakes, you can see cider pressing demonstrations on a vintage press, watch celebrity chefs cook with cider, examine a wide variety of apples, or simply head to the marquee on the lawn that serves a selection of Wales' best ciders and perrys. But get there early – this event is incredibly popular and the biggest challenge of the day is finding somewhere to park.

The Cider Year: Apple Day

Autumn is the time of harvest, and that's something that has always been celebrated by festivals. In 1990 Sue Clifford and Angela King decided to create a new one of their own. The storming success of French Golden Delicious apples had prompted the British apple industry to move towards a more monocultural crop of its own, something standardised that pleased the largest number of people and offended no one. Sue and Angela felt that the great diversity of apples was under threat, which in turn threatened the rest of the life that teems in our orchards. Apple Day – a harvest-time celebration of the orchard – aimed to rectify that by helping people remember their relationship with nature.

The beauty of the idea is its simplicity, which allowed it to spread with amazing speed. Apple Days are now held across the UK on the closest weekend to 21st October. Some are small community events in schools or church halls. Others are lavish affairs in stately homes or large orchards. Some are simply about the fruit itself, with apple bobbing and toffee apples, and displays of the many different apple varieties that are now grown. But the best ones – of course – also involve cider. If you pick the right Apple Day event there is often a wide range of ciders available – purely to help demonstrate the apple in all its glory you understand. And there are many of these across Wales. October need never be boring again.

GOWER CIDER WEEKEND

(Mid-October)
Gower Heritage Centre
www.gowerheritagecentre.co.uk

The old nineteenth century cider press grinds into action once again as the Gower Heritage Centre gives a demonstration of how cider is made, from the growing of the apples to the pouring of a pint. With around fifteen Welsh ciders to choose from, there are also craft stalls, a barbeque and live music. If you miss the mad magic of the cheese and cider festival in May, here's another chance to be amazed.

LLANERCHAERON APPLE WEEK

(Early October)
Ciliau Aeron, nr Aberaeron,
Pembrokeshire SA48 8DG
www.nationaltrust.org.uk/llanerchaeron

This eighteenth century Welsh estate has a walled garden and a small farm, and is owned by the National Trust. Apple festivals feature activities for all the family as well as cider.

APPLE WEEKEND AT NATIONAL BOTANIC GARDEN OF WALES

(Late October)
Llanarthne, Carmarthenshire SA32 8HG
www.gardenofwales.org.uk

Hundreds of apple varieties are available to ogle at or even sample as well as stalls selling everything apple-related, from pies and pork, cheese and chutney, to cider and squash. There are also plenty of family activities such as apple pressing and making your own juice.

Cider and Perry and Fabulous Food

It's only convention that tells us wine is the drink we should have to accompany food. We only think this because our ideas about fine dining are heavily influenced by the French.

In truth, if you're looking for the very best flavour matches, the pairings that really transform a meal, there is no 'should' about it, just a constant quest to find the perfect pairing. It might be based on pure flavour, or tradition, or terroir. Not even the French accompany food with wine all the time: go to Normandy or Brittany, and you'll find the default drink with food is cider. We think it's time that was more common in Wales too.

> If you're looking for the very best flavour matches, the pairings that really transform a meal, there is no 'should' about it, just a constant quest to find the perfect pairing.

The perfect match

There are no rules about matching food and drink, but there are some guidelines that tend to work. When pairing, you're looking for at least one of three things:

- Flavours that harmonise and complement each other
- Flavours that contrast with each other
- Something that cuts through strong flavour or texture, refreshing the palate.

Cider can be great at all three. For flavours that harmonise, think about the kind of food that apples go with, and cider will work too. That iconic image of an apple stuffed into the mouth of a boar's head is a big clue that cider was made to go with anything pork-based. There's a sweetness in pork that works beautifully with the fruity character of cider. Light, delicate ciders, and particularly good perrys, are also great with seafood.

For contrast, again think logically. For instance, the way we often temper the heat of a curry with a fruity chutney suggests a sweet cider will have the same effect and it does – so long as the cider isn't too tannic.

Fire & Ice
Narberth
Ultimate Cider Sorbet
Made With
100% Welsh Whole Juice Cider
&
Welsh Cider Apple Juice
Over 18's Only

The acidity in cider cuts through anything creamy. And if it's carbonated, cider will break through anything fatty, cleansing the palate. These are just some of the reasons why cider goes amazingly well with cheese.

If you want to round out your meal to be a banquet to remember, sparkling perry or cider served in champagne flutes is a more than worthy substitute for the French stuff. Herefordshire cider makers invented the *méthode champenoise* a century before the French claimed it, and for our money the best perrys beat champers at its own game.

At the other end of the meal, cider brandy makes a wonderful *digestif*.

Because we're accustomed to thinking of cider in relation to beer, when we see something that's 7% ABV we tend to regard it as 'rocket fuel', something that will put us on our backs after a couple of pints. It might be more helpful to compare ciders of this strength to wine instead. The strength of wine is increasing, and now averages 13.5% ABV. Switch to cider instead, and suddenly that 7% ABV beverage, sipped from wine glasses, is a responsible drinking choice, delivering all the flavour of wine with half the alcohol.

Cooking with cider

Just like wine, cider can also be a wonderful ingredient in food. As part of a sauce or stock, it enhances other flavours. You can't go wrong with any pork, poultry or game stew with cider. Cooking clams or mussels in cider brings out an amazing seaside freshness – *moules marinieres* with cider instead of white wine is so heavenly that it will surely be made illegal if too many people find out about it.

As with matching, wherever apples go, cider can go too. But with cider's breadth of character, from sweet to acidic to dry or tannic, it's incredibly flexible. It can also be a dressing or a marinade. Cider vinegar is already popular in this role, (not to mention being the latest Hollywood health fad), and deservedly so, but straight cider with good acidity offers a softer alternative. An apple and bacon salad with a cider dressing brings together everything we've been talking about, transporting you to cider heaven.

The only watch-out when cooking with cider is to be wary of clashes between tannins and spices. Apart from that, the joy is in experimenting: not everything will hit the same peaks, but it's difficult to do something that goes completely wrong, and rare indeed that cider doesn't enhance a dish in some way.

Give it a go!

One of the many beautiful things about cider is that it is so much cheaper than wine. While wine can be intimidating and scary, cider is lower risk. If you want to try matching, you could buy a few different ciders and a few lumps of varied cheese and have a fun and different evening doing a cider and cheese matching for six or eight people for little more than £20. If there's anything that really doesn't work with one, it will probably go with another, and if it doesn't, you haven't wasted much. If you want to experiment more generally matching cider with anything from barbecue and takeaway through to fine dining, even if the cider doesn't go with the food, it'll taste perfectly nice on its own a day or so later.

And cooking with cider really couldn't be simpler. It's very unlikely a splash of cider will spoil a dish, and highly likely that it will improve it. What have you got to lose? Whether it's a one-pot stew outside a tent on a camping holiday in the hills or a dinner party back home in a smart kitchen, the principles above are all you need to start using cider and cider vinegar as a transformative ingredient.

If you're still not sure, here are a couple of tried and tested recipes to start you off. Trust us, once you've made these, there'll be no stopping you.

Pickled Mushrooms in Cider Vinegar

We had a play around with some recipes and have come up with your new favourite store cupboard staple; this uses a good local cider vinegar.

Ingredients

1kg 'meaty' mushrooms, such as ceps, oyster and button
500ml cider vinegar
200g sugar
2 tsp sea salt
2 garlic cloves, peeled & roughly crushed
1 red chilli, sliced in half lengthways
1 tbsp dried oregano
A couple of bay leaves

Method

Wash the mushrooms and place in a pan with a tight fitting lid. Put the cider vinegar, salt, sugar, garlic and chilli in another pan, and bring to the boil over a medium heat. Allow to simmer for a couple of minutes, then add the oregano and bay leaves. Pour over the mushrooms, put the lid on and leave it to one side to cool.

When cool, divide the mushrooms and the liquid into clean sterilised jars and seal. Leave for at least 2 weeks in the fridge before opening, and then serve as an accompaniment to salads, or indeed anything else you fancy. Will keep in the fridge for up to 6 months.

Laverbread, Bacon, Cockles and Fried Bread

Serves 4

This recipe doesn't contain cider, but we found that it goes well with a glass of your favourite tipple, and is the perfect meal to pull together on your camping stove when you're visiting the beautiful Welsh coast.
If you want the full flavour of the cider, add in a good dash when you are cooking the cockles with the laverbread.

Ingredients

200 g cockle meat (or 350 g fresh cockles)
4 x 120-150 g thick bacon or gammon slices
250 g laverbread
2 knobs butter
1tbsp cooking oil
1 tsp salt
4 slices of bread that is a couple of days old

Method

Preheat a lightly oiled grill or griddle pan and cook the bacon/gammon for 4-5 minutes on each side, until browned and cooked through.

Meanwhile, put the laverbread into a pan with a knob of butter and gently fry. Throw in the cockle meat, and fry for a further few minutes on a low heat. (If you are using fresh cockles, you will need to clean and steam them until they are cooked before tossing through the laverbread).

In a separate pan, heat to a medium heat and cover the base with oil & butter. Add the bread and cook for 2-3 minutes each side until crispy and golden.

Spoon the laverbread and cockle mix on to 4 serving plates, place a bacon/gammon on each and serve with the fried bread.

Welsh Cider and Chorizo by Sian Bassett Roberts

Sian is a Welsh Food Promoter and Director of Coginio. As a company, Coginio has produced the 'Coginio' series of Welsh Cooking DVDs, the luxury cookery break, 'Egwyl Fwyd Blas ar Gymru/Taste of Wales Cookery Break' and runs a variety of Welsh Food presentations, workshops and demonstrations.

Ingredients

Olive oil
300 ml cider
1 bay leaf
3 Chorizo sausages
1 apple (sweet)

Method

Slice the chorizo sausages into half inch segments

Pour a little olive oil into a pan and heat

Add chorizo and cook for 1 minute each side on a low heat

Slice the apple into 12 segments

Add the apple, bay leaf, and cider – turn up the heat and cook until the cider begins to thicken.

Serve hot with cocktail sticks.

Cider Apple Cake with Streusel Topping, by Nerys Howell

Nerys Howell is a food author, home economist and TV chef and runs a food consultancy business in Cardiff. She has travelled widely promoting Welsh food and drink across the world and believes passionately in the quality of the food and drink produced in Wales. Her book, Wales on a Plate brings to life the traditions, lifestyles and cooking of Wales combined with Nerys' more contemporary recipes based on produce from the land, river and coast of Wales.

Serves: 12

Preparation time: 30 minutes + marinating overnight

Cooking time: 50-60 minutes

Ingredients

175g large raisins

200ml cider

175g self raising flour

1 teaspoon baking powder

1 teaspoon ground cinnamon

110g soft butter

110g demerara sugar

2 large eggs

2 tablespoons whole milk

2 tablespoons cider left over from marinating raisins

1 large cooking apple, about 225g in weight, peeled and diced

Topping

75g self raising flour
25g butter
50g demerara sugar
50g whole almonds halved lengthways

Method

Soak the raisins in the cider overnight or alternatively (if you are in a hurry) put the raisins and the cider in a small saucepan and simmer gently for about 20 minutes until the raisins are plump and have absorbed the cider. Set aside to cool and pour out any cider left over and keep to one side. Sift the flour and baking powder into a bowl, add the rest of the cake ingredients (except the apple and cider) and using an electric hand whisk or a wooden spoon beat the mixture until smooth. Fold in the apple and raisins and if the mixture is too dry add some of the remaining cider and milk. Spoon the mixture into a 20cm spring form tin which has been greased and lined with greaseproof paper.

To prepare the topping, place the flour and butter into a small bowl and rub in until the mixture resembles breadcrumbs. Add the sugar, mixing it in evenly then sprinkle in a dessertspoon of the reserved cider. Sprinkle this mixture on top of the cake and arrange the almonds evenly over the surface. Bake in the centre of a preheated oven 180°C/Gas mark 4 for 50-60 minutes until cooked through. Leave to cool in the tin for 30 minutes before turning out on a wire rack. Sieve icing sugar over the surface before serving.

Cider Trails

Welsh cider makers and great cider pubs are somewhat spread out and rural, so a car, or at least a bike, is essential. Given that cider is an intoxicating substance, we cannot recommend an intense trail of cider visits unless you're with someone who is happy to drive and not drink. So seeking out Welsh cider is something that has to be done at a leisurely pace, and is no worse for that in a region blessed with wonderful campsites and B&Bs.

Here are two ideas for short cider breaks which we have tried and tested. For extra value, try timing them with a food and drink or cider festival.

South Wales

The pretty market town of Abergavenny is a perfect base to visit Wales' busiest cider region. The Angel Hotel (www.angelabergavenny.com) is perfect if you're looking to splash out, or there are cheaper B&Bs in town and a range of campsites just outside.

Head ten minutes out of town towards Raglan on the A40 for lunch at the Clytha Arms (p64). Do this late on Friday or a Sunday afternoon, phone ahead, and you might then catch the Cider House at Raglan Cider Mill (p61) just around the corner. Carry on the A40 to Monmouth and from there head north on the B4233 through Rockfield, possibly pausing at Stonemill (p66) and then onto the B4347. This will take you to Ty Gwyn, (p42) whose farm shop is open to the public. From there, head up to the junction with the B4521, turn right and you're almost immediately at the Bell at Skenfrith (p63). This road, the Old Ross Road, will take you back to Abergavenny in twenty minutes.

Out of town towards Brecon, you have the Nantyffin Cider Mill (p59) and then the Bacchus off-licence in Crickhowell (p67) just a few minutes away.

Do this on the right weekend in September and a host of cider makers will be waiting for you back in town at the Abergavenny Food Festival (p84).

And if you're leaving the area via the M4, make sure you build in time to pop into the Bell at Caerleon (p63) on your way back.

North Wales

There's no better base of operations for a visit around North Wales cider makers than the Blue Bell Inn at Halkyn (p54). Landlord Steve Marquis will give you all the help, advice, directions and introductions you need. The Blue Bell does not offer accommodation, but a few minutes walk down the road is the wonderful North Wales Buffalo Bed & Breakfast – yes, that's right – a buffalo farm that offers B&B, not to mention stunning views from the Halkyn Mountain all the way across what looks like half of northern England (www.buffalo-meat.co.uk). From here a number of cider makers such as Dee Ciders (p30) and Rosie's Triple D (p31) are very close, as are wonderful cider pubs such as the Bridge End Inn (p55) and the Penrhyn Arms (p56). We visited on the weekend of Apple Day at Erdigg Hall (p86) for added interest.

Glossary

ABV: Alcohol by Volume, the percentage of alcohol in a given drink. Craft cider is commonly around 6-8% ABV.

Bottle conditioning: process whereby carbonation is naturally attained by keeping residual yeast in the bottle, which produces CO2 for a natural sparkle.

Champenoise (Méthode): refined method of bottle conditioning with the addition of champagne yeasts, which produces a clear, naturally sparkling drink. Commonly associated with Champagne, it is also widely used in cider and was in fact invented in the seventeenth century by Herefordshire cider makers.

Cider: alcoholic drink created by the fermentation of apple juice. The equivalent for apples of what wine is to grapes.

Craft Cider: an imprecise term which generally implies a high quality, all-juice cider produced artisanally on a small scale.

Fermentation: the process whereby yeast turns sugar into alcohol.

Maceration: process whereby milled apple or pear pulp is left to oxidise prior to pressing and fermentation, which can create deeper, richer flavours.

Perai: the Welsh word for perry.

Perry: alcoholic drink created by the fermentation of pear juice. The equivalent for pears of what wine is to grapes.

Pomace: the flesh of milled, crushed apples.

Press: equipment which extracts juice from pomace.

Real Cider: term developed by CAMRA to indicate cider that is pure 100% pressed juice with no additives or preservatives and no artificial carbonation.

Scratter: equipment for chopping up whole apples into a mush so they can be pressed. A more modern equivalent to the traditional cider mill.

Scrumpy: imprecise term often used interchangeably with real cider – 100% fresh pressed juice with no additives, fermented with wild yeast which can give it funky, farmyard notes. Also referred to as farmhouse cider.

Seidr: the Welsh word for cider.

Tannin: chemical compound which occurs in cider apples, giving dryness, bitterness and/or astringency.

Wassail: winter festival when orchards are celebrated and trees are encouraged to wake up after their winter slumber by drink-fuelled rituals.

Yeast: a microscopic organism that's all around us. Yeast eats sugar and produces alcohol and carbon dixide. The basis for fermentation, it occurs naturally in apples.

Useful Contacts

Welsh Perry and Cider Society

The Office, Blaengawney Farm, Mynydd Maen,
Hafodyrynys, Crumlin, Caerphilly NP11 5AY
01495 240983
info@welshcider.co.uk
www.welshcider.co.uk

For everything you wanted to know about Welsh cider
and perry but didn't know who to ask.

Visit Wales

08708 300 306
info@visitwales.co.uk
www.visitwales.co.uk

Your first port of call when planning a trip to Wales.
Full information on travel, accommodation and ideas for
things to see and do if, for some reason, visiting cider
makers and drinking ciders is not enough.

The Official Gateway to Wales

www.wales.com

Loads of information about history, culture and visiting
Wales.

Hereford Cider Museum

Pomona Place, Hereford HR4 0EF
enquiries@cidermuseum.co.uk
01432 354207
www.cidermuseum.co.uk

Not quite in Wales, but well worth popping over the
border for. The UK's leading cider exhibit tells the
history of cider making in Wales as well as England.

The Campaign for Real Ale (CAMRA)

230 Hatfield Road, St Albans, AL1 4LW
01727 867201
camra@camra.org.uk
www.camra.org.uk

Their definition of 'real cider' may be a bit too narrow
for us, but no one does more across the UK to
champion cider as well as real ale.

The National Association of Cider Makers (NACM)

c/o International Wine & Spirit Centre -39-45
Bermondsey Street, London SE1 3XF
info@cideruk.com
www.cideruk.com

The official trade body for the UK cider industry.